Janet Holmes

nest

*rescued chickens
at home*

KEHRER

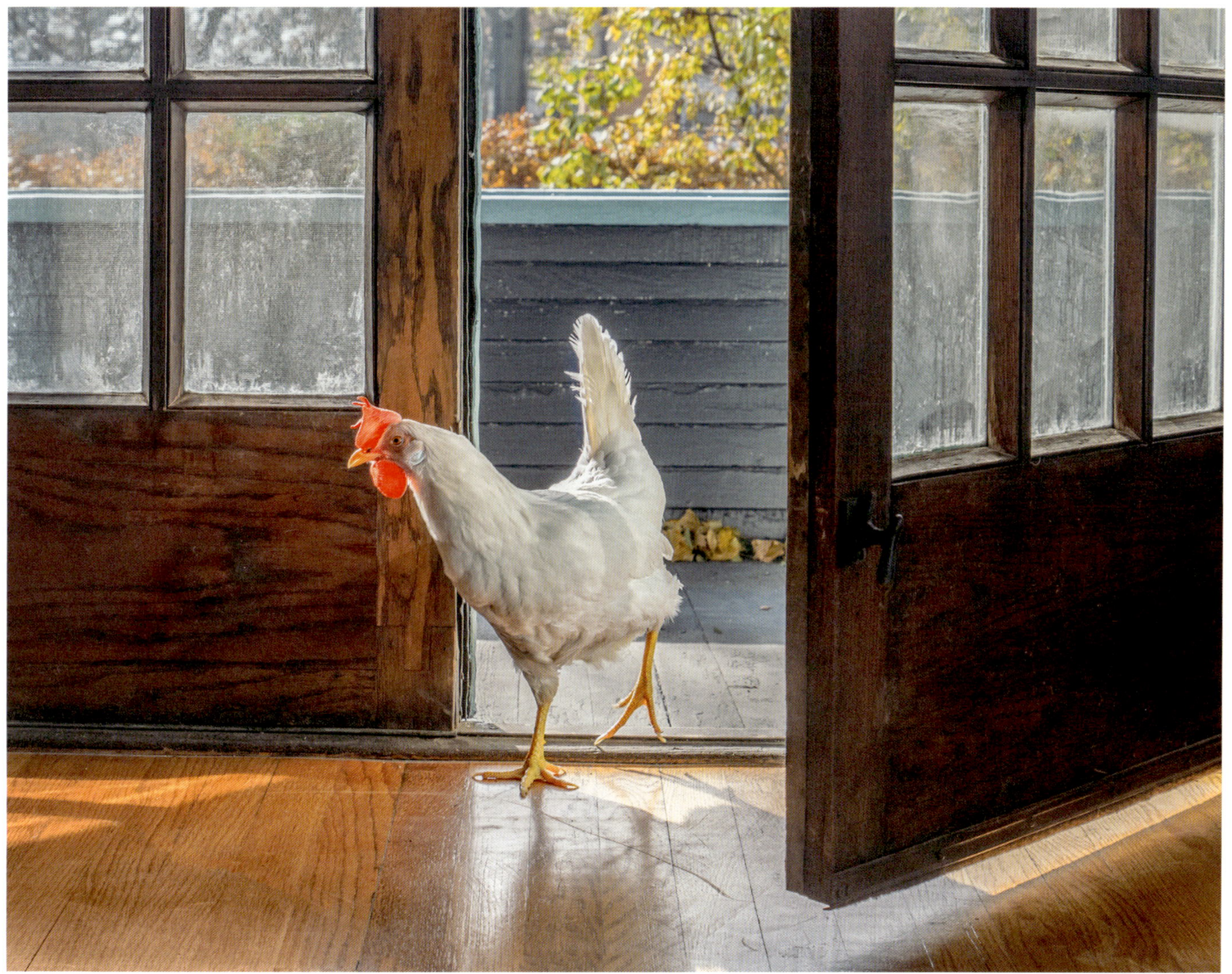

Winnie

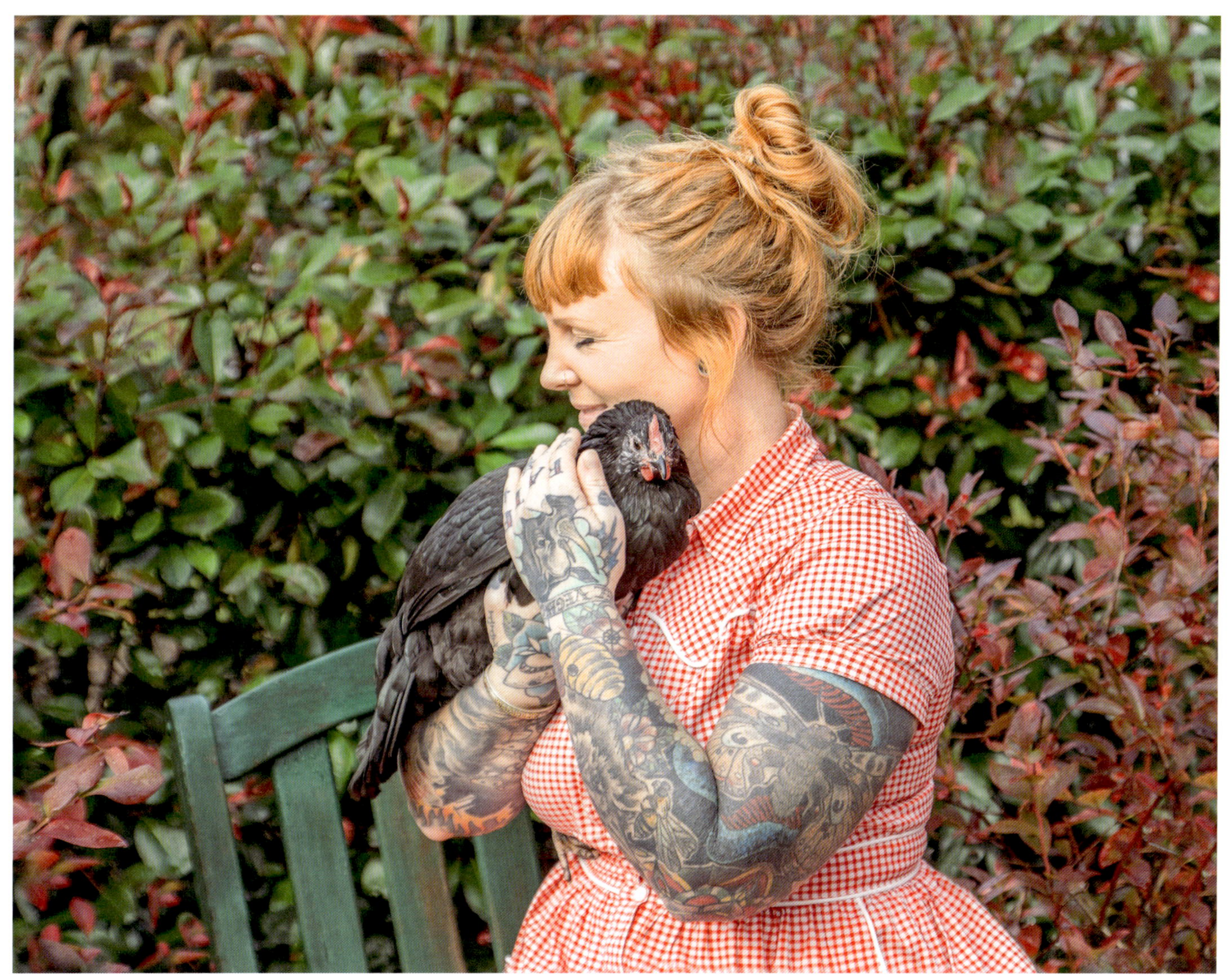

Emily and Jenny

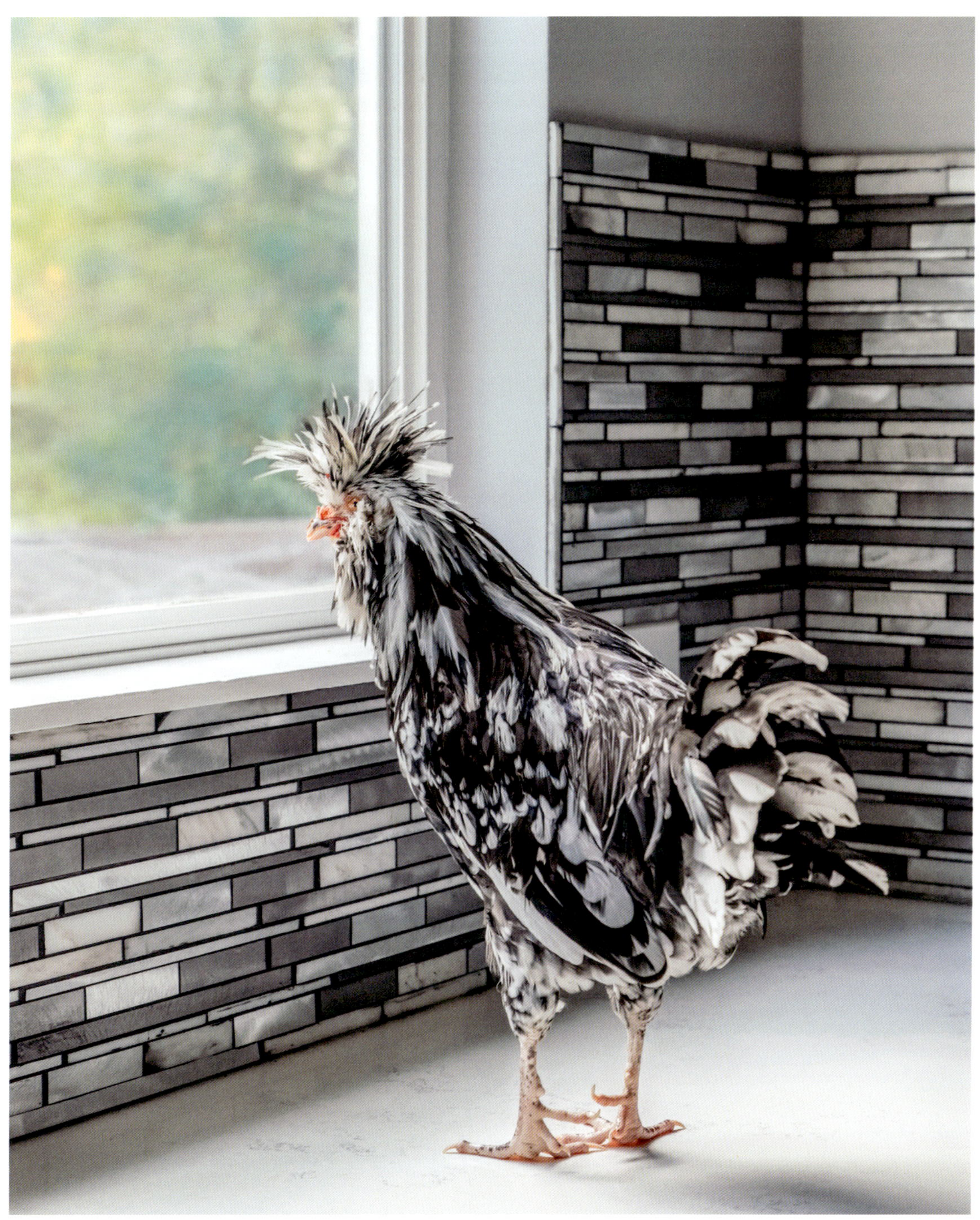

Jon Snow

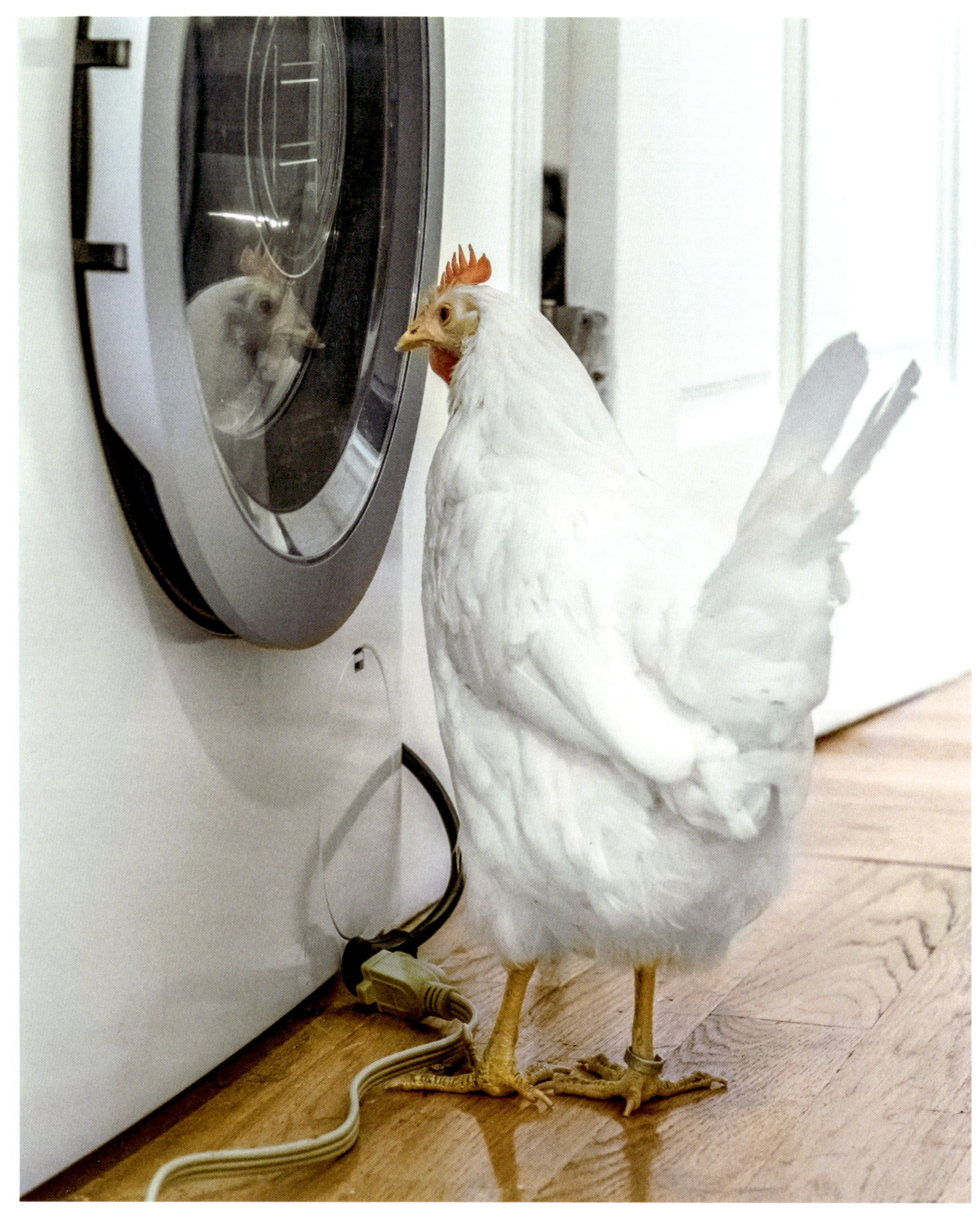

Dualla

How do we decide which animals are family, and which are food? Why are we surprised to see a rooster gazing out the kitchen window or a hen investigating the laundry? After all, chickens are present in most homes, as flesh and eggs, rather than as individuals with personalities of their own.

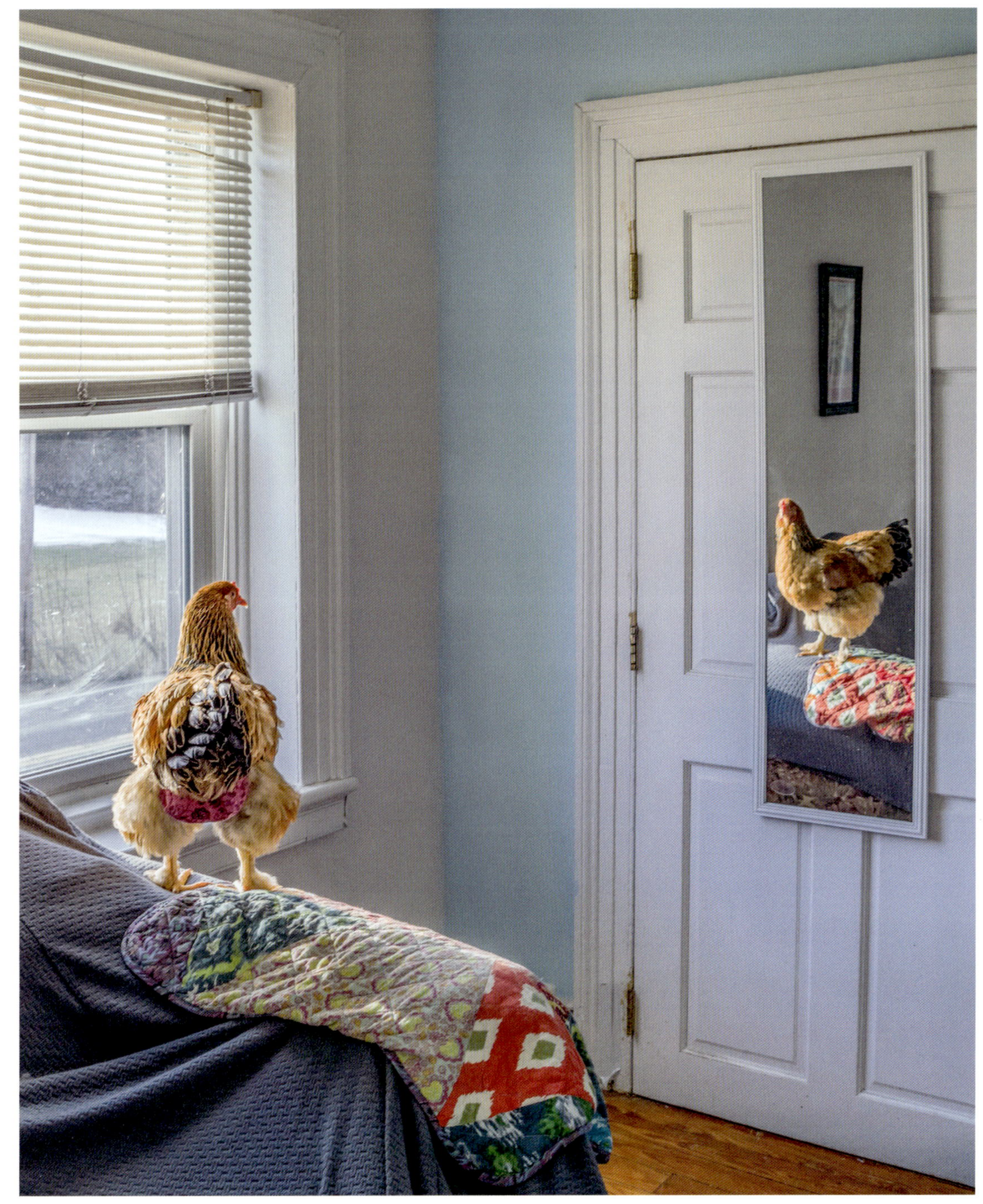

Asa

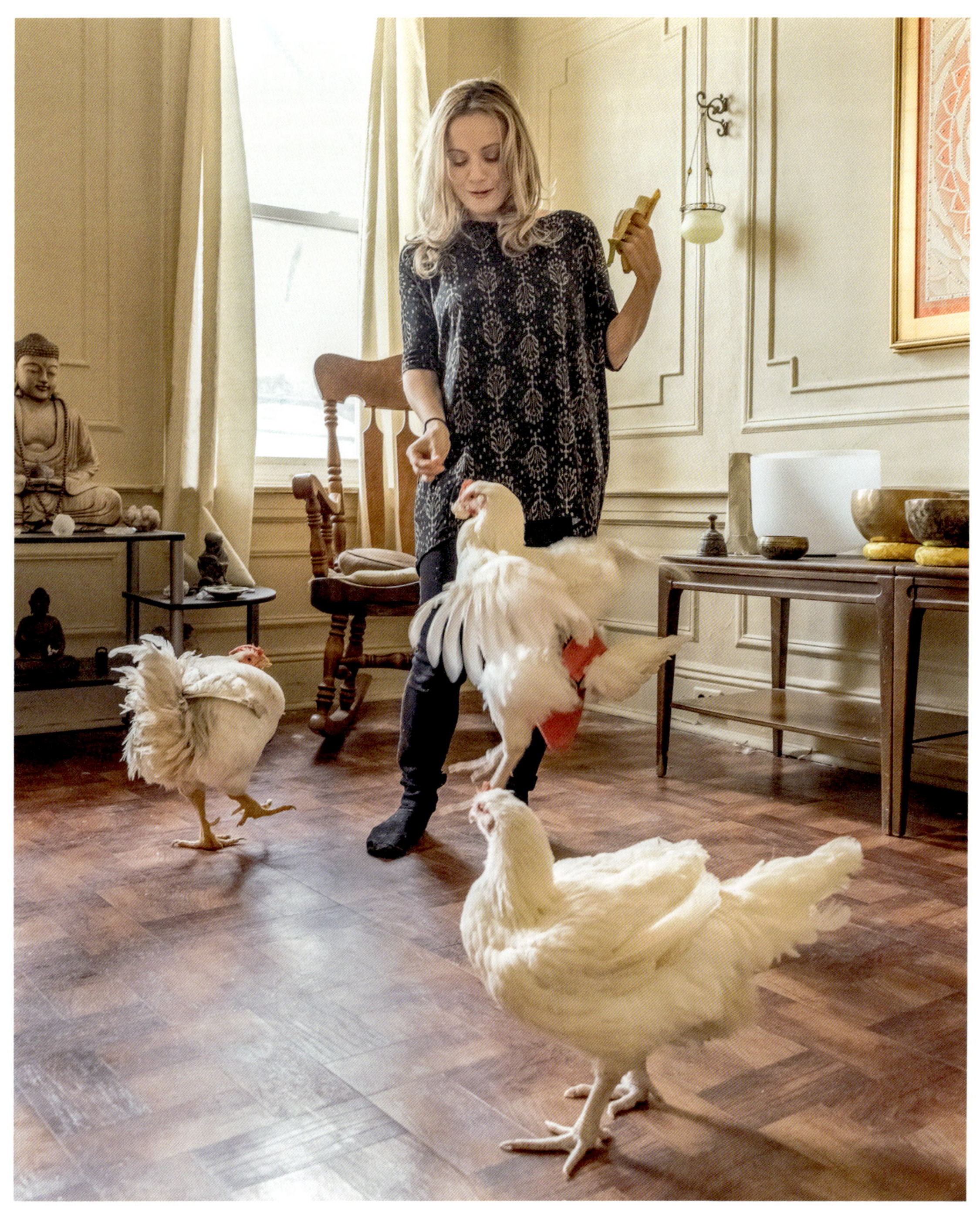

Penelope, Vanessa, Alicia, and Jenny

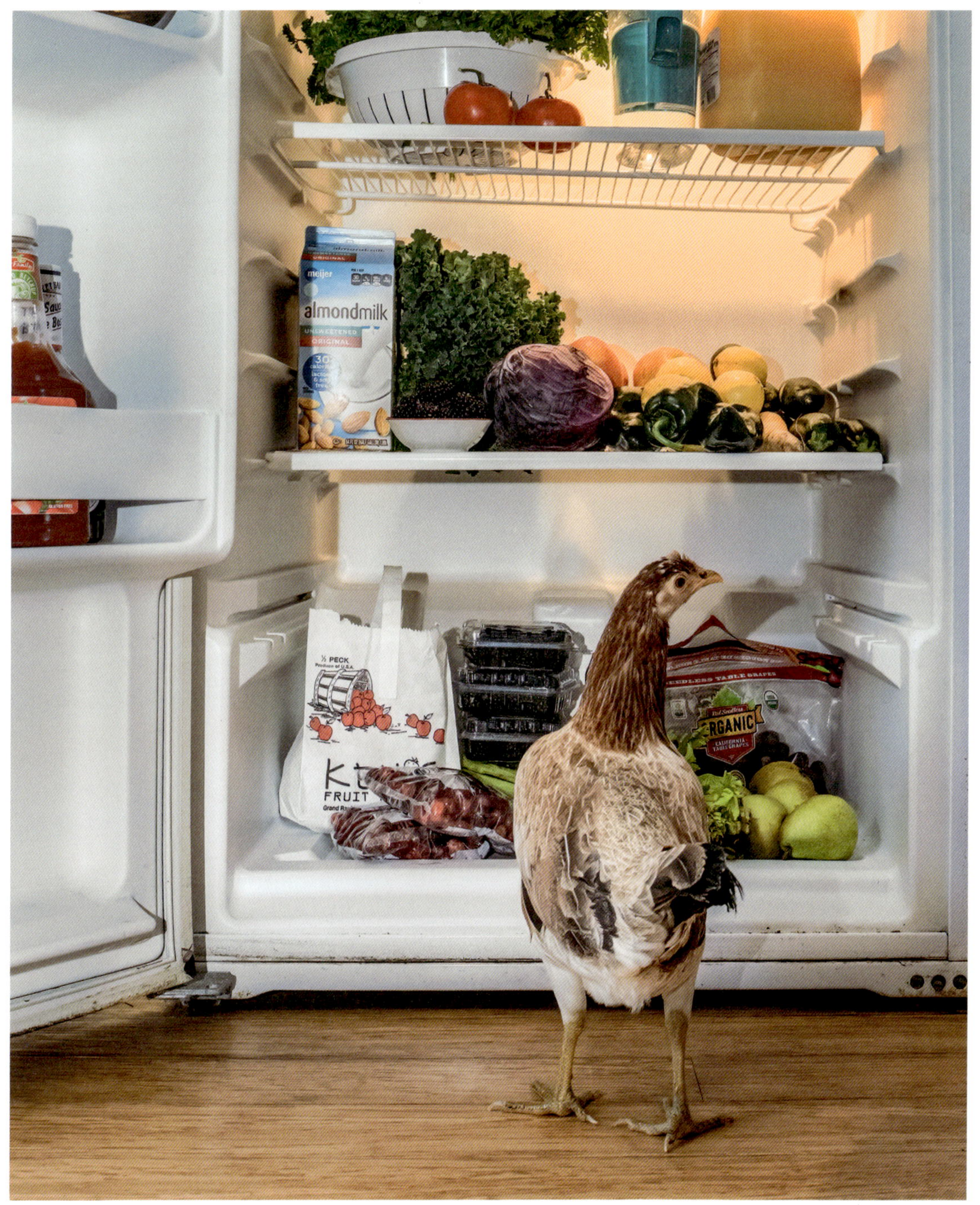

Cluckey

Introduction

I've always loved animals, but for many years I was afraid to get involved with rescuing them because I didn't think I could handle the heartbreak. I was almost fifty when I finally acknowledged that animals needed me more than I needed to be comfortable. And so I began volunteering with rescue groups as a caregiver and photographer.

One of those groups was the Wild Bird Fund in New York City, where, a few years later, I helped care for a hen suffering from severe and chronic reproductive illness. Once the hen was no longer acutely ill, she needed to find a sanctuary or private home where she could get regular (and expensive) veterinary care to manage her illness. I began contacting my friends at farm animal sanctuaries and, in doing so, was introduced to a network of people (primarily vegan women) who rescue and care for chickens in their homes.

I thought about how so many women still struggle to obtain adequate, affordable reproductive health care and how in turn, we have been socialized to exploit hens' reproductive systems. This parallel inspired me to begin photographing chickens and their rescuers to honor the bonds between them.

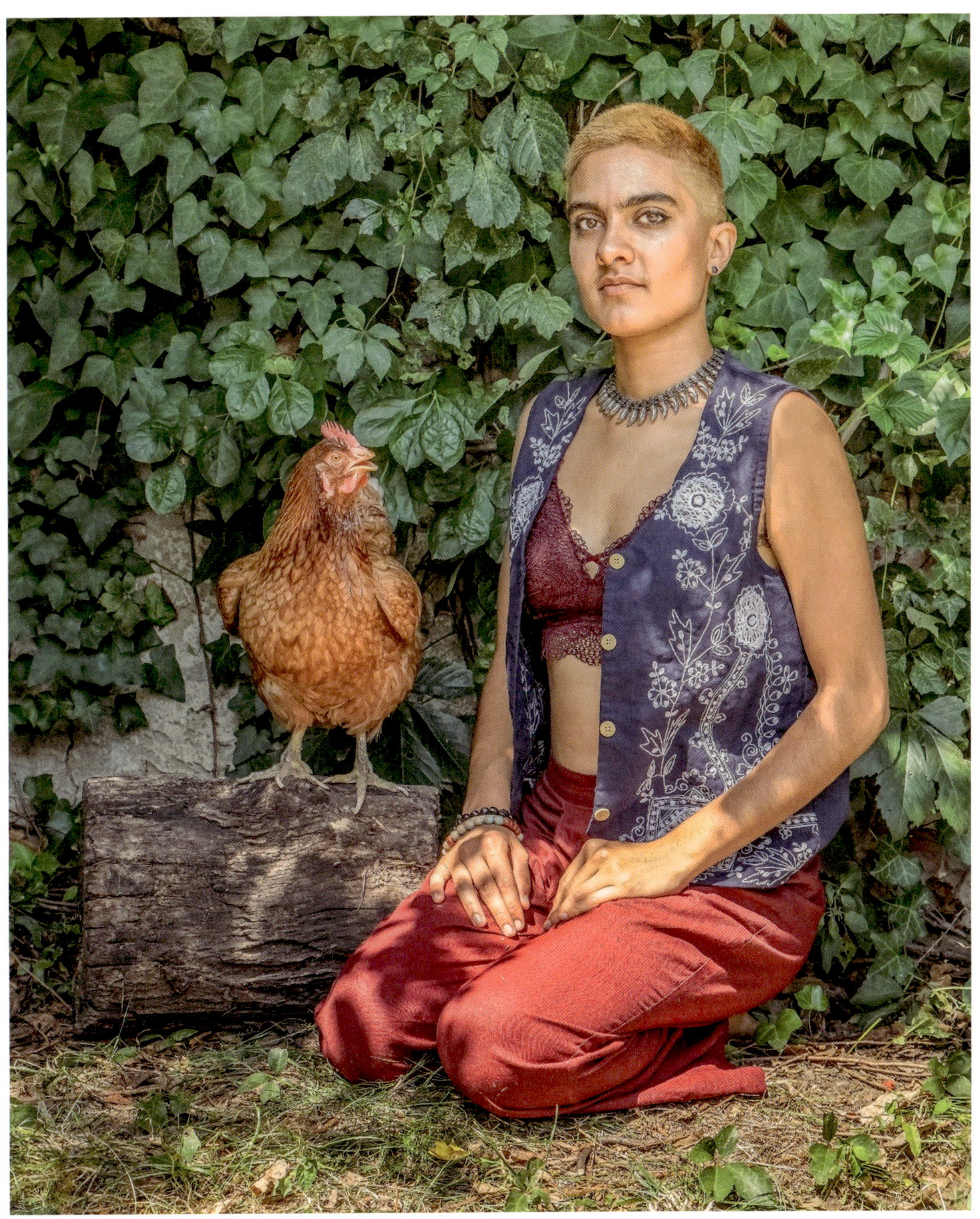

Corrie and Mahika

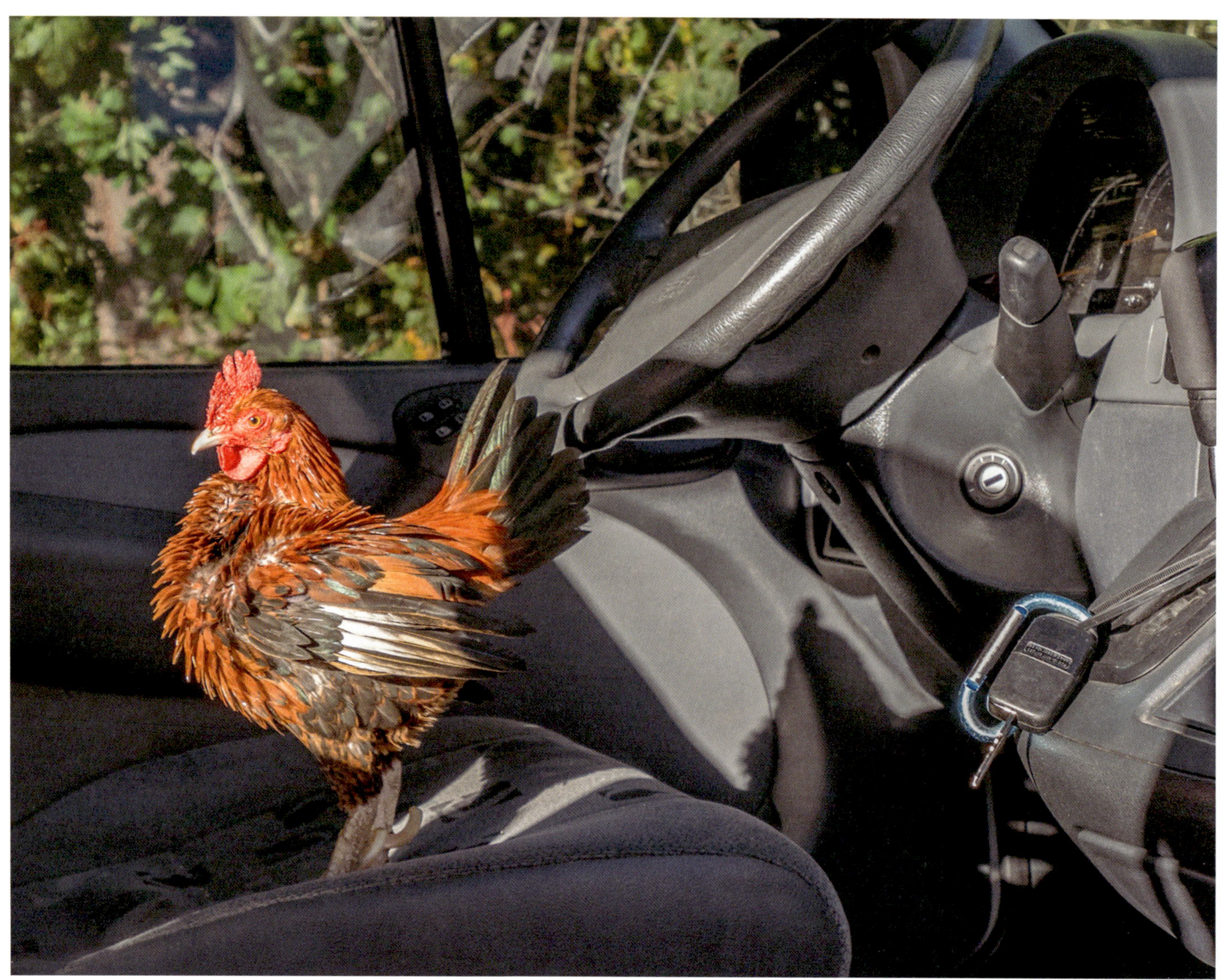

Chicken Little

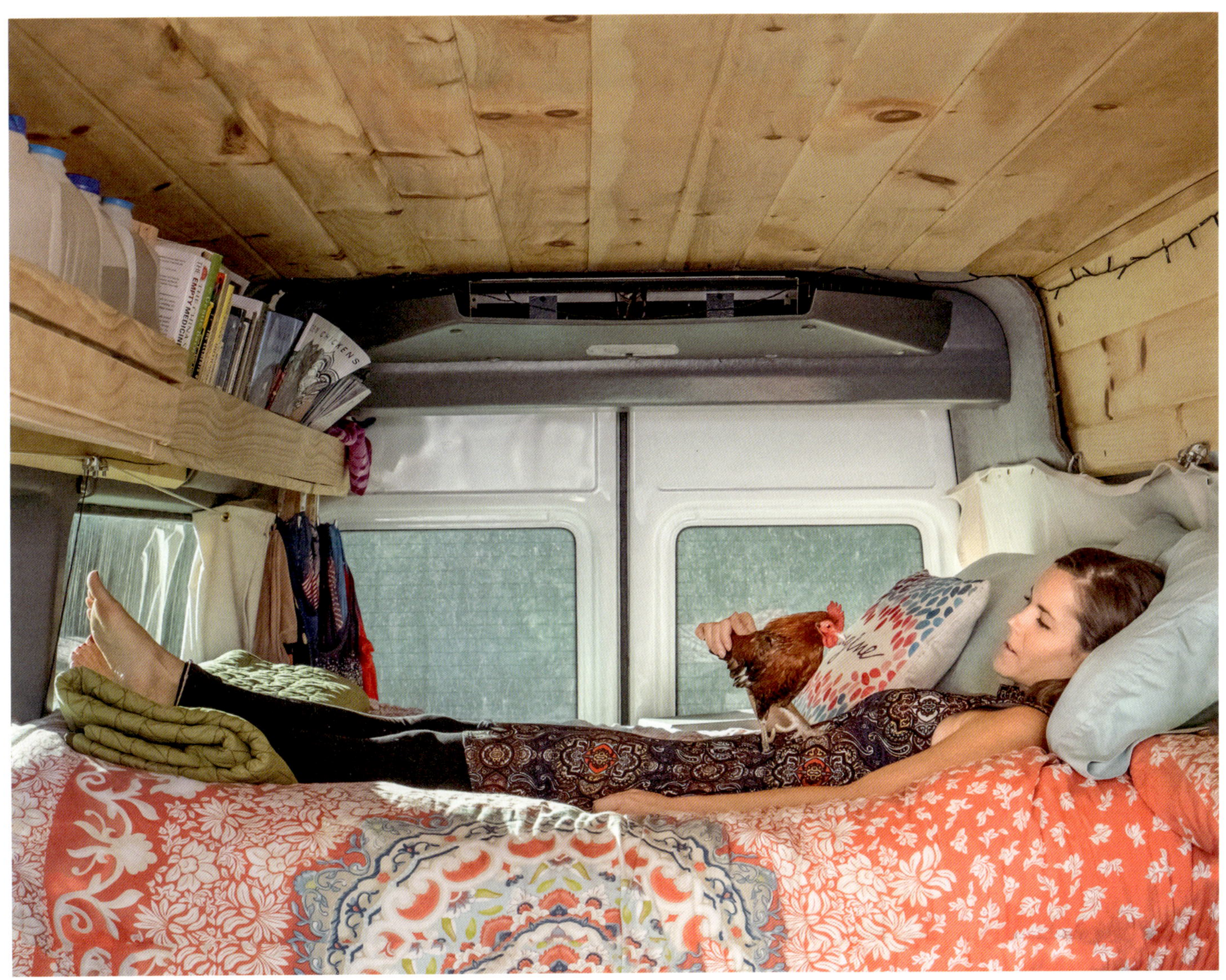

Chicken Little and Jessica

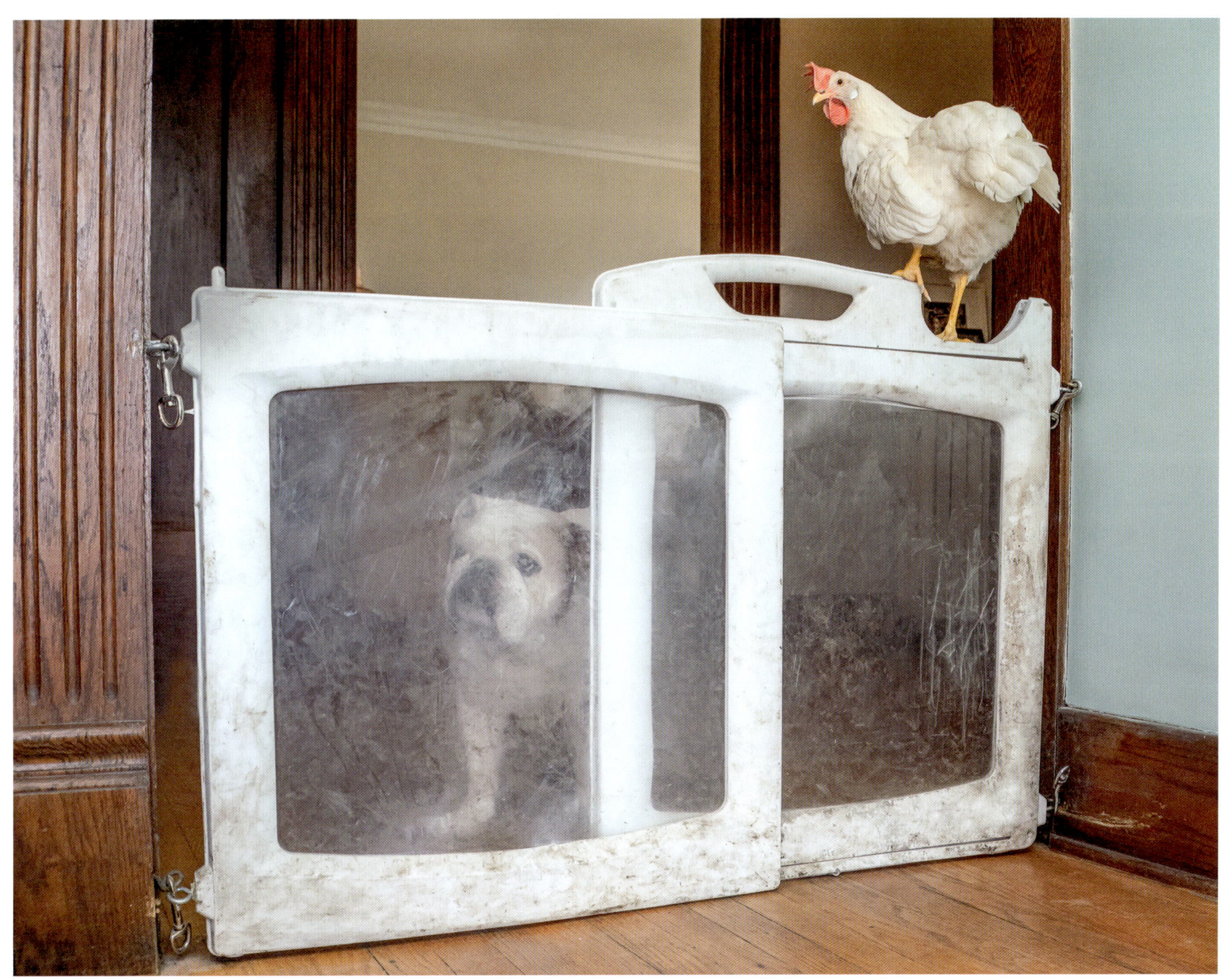

Dee Dee and Winnie

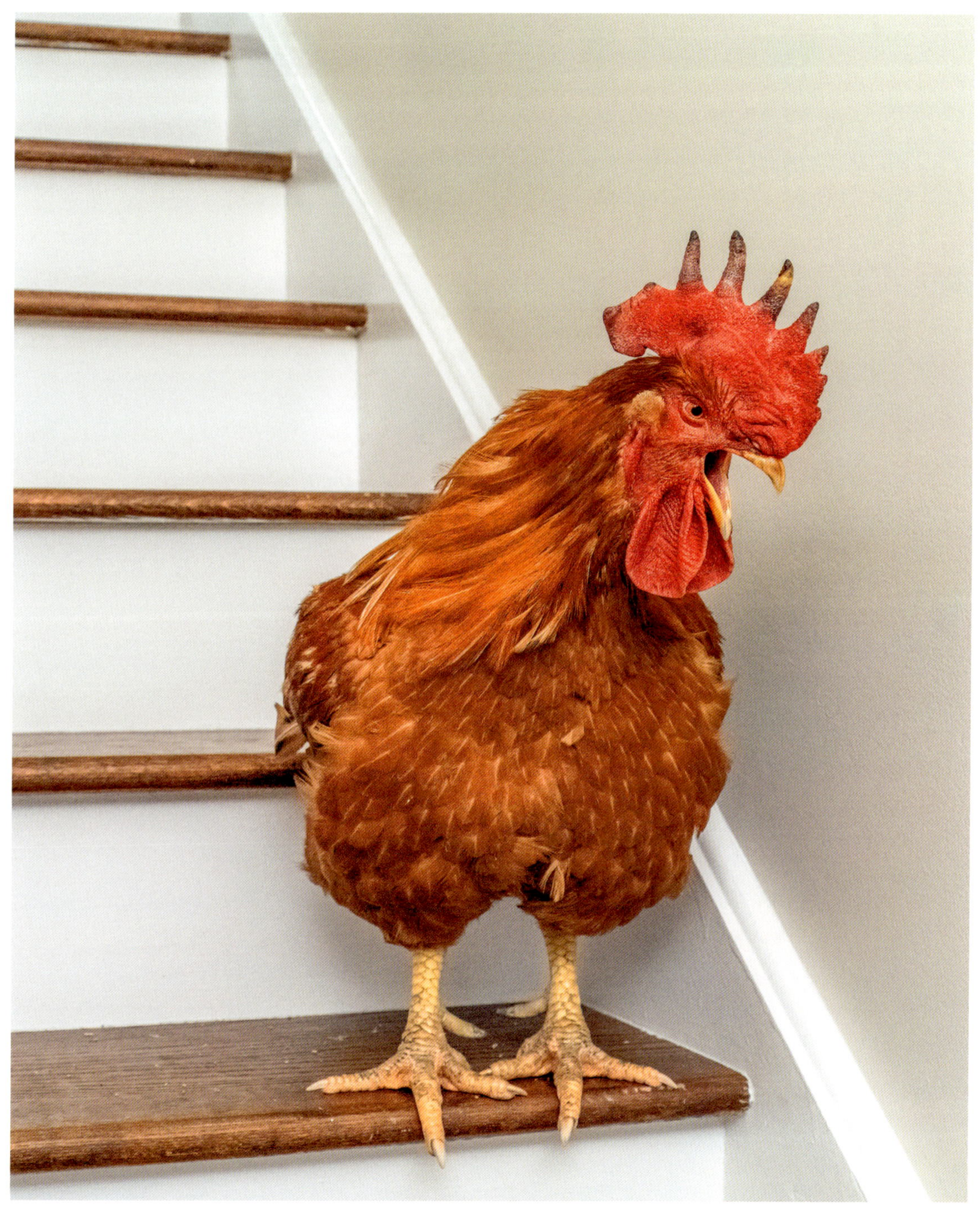

Leonard Crowen

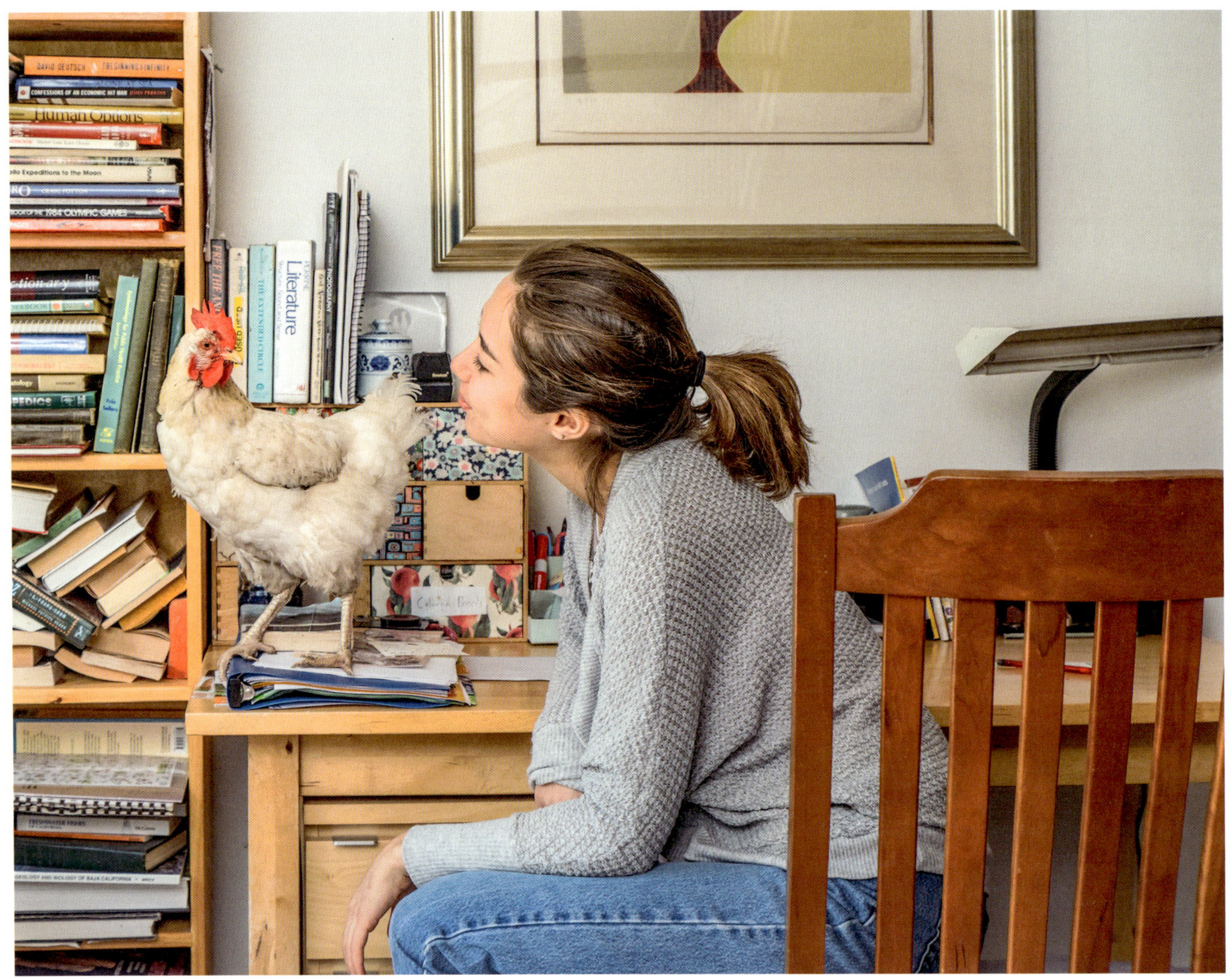

Pearl and Rachel

Unlike their wild ancestors, who laid about twelve to twenty eggs each spring, most modern hens have been bred and then manipulated to produce hundreds of eggs throughout the year. Under pressure to lay the large eggs that we enjoy eating, their bodies break down quickly. Depleted of essential nutrients like calcium, these hens can't form shells around all of their eggs, so their bodies become full of egg matter that rots or binds their organs together. They suffer from prolapsed uteruses and sometimes bleed to death. Accelerated cell division associated with so much egg-laying also substantially increases their risk of reproductive cancer.

In fetid battery cages and crowded barns, they can hardly move, occupying a space that is, on average, about the size of a page in this book. Their bodies leached of calcium from non-stop egg-laying, they develop osteoporosis and, when their bones break, they collapse and are trampled to death by their neighbors.

If they survive to reach their second birthday, they are likely to be killed soon afterward as their egg production slows down. This is far short of the ten to thirty-year lifespan of their wild ancestors.

Even backyard hens produce far more eggs than their bodies can handle. They might live in healthier environments with people who care about them, but they suffer from many of the same health problems as factory-raised birds. As prey animals, chickens often avoid any appearance of illness until it is too late to save them.

Reproductive health care services for hens can be very hard to find, since few veterinarians are experienced in providing such care. When it is available, it is often costly. Treatment through hormonal implants, which can stop egg-laying, can cost several hundred dollars per treatment and may only be effective for three to nine months. Treatment of acute illness (for example, to drain an abdomen full of egg matter, correct prolapsed organs or remove fallopian tubes) can cost thousands of dollars.

With adequate veterinary care, healthy diets, secure habitats, and loving companionship, hens sometimes live for several years. But often, their bodies have been so compromised by selective breeding and their experiences before being rescued that they only live for a few weeks or months with their caregivers. At least they get to spend their last days in a comfortable and safe place, surrounded by love.

Janet Holmes

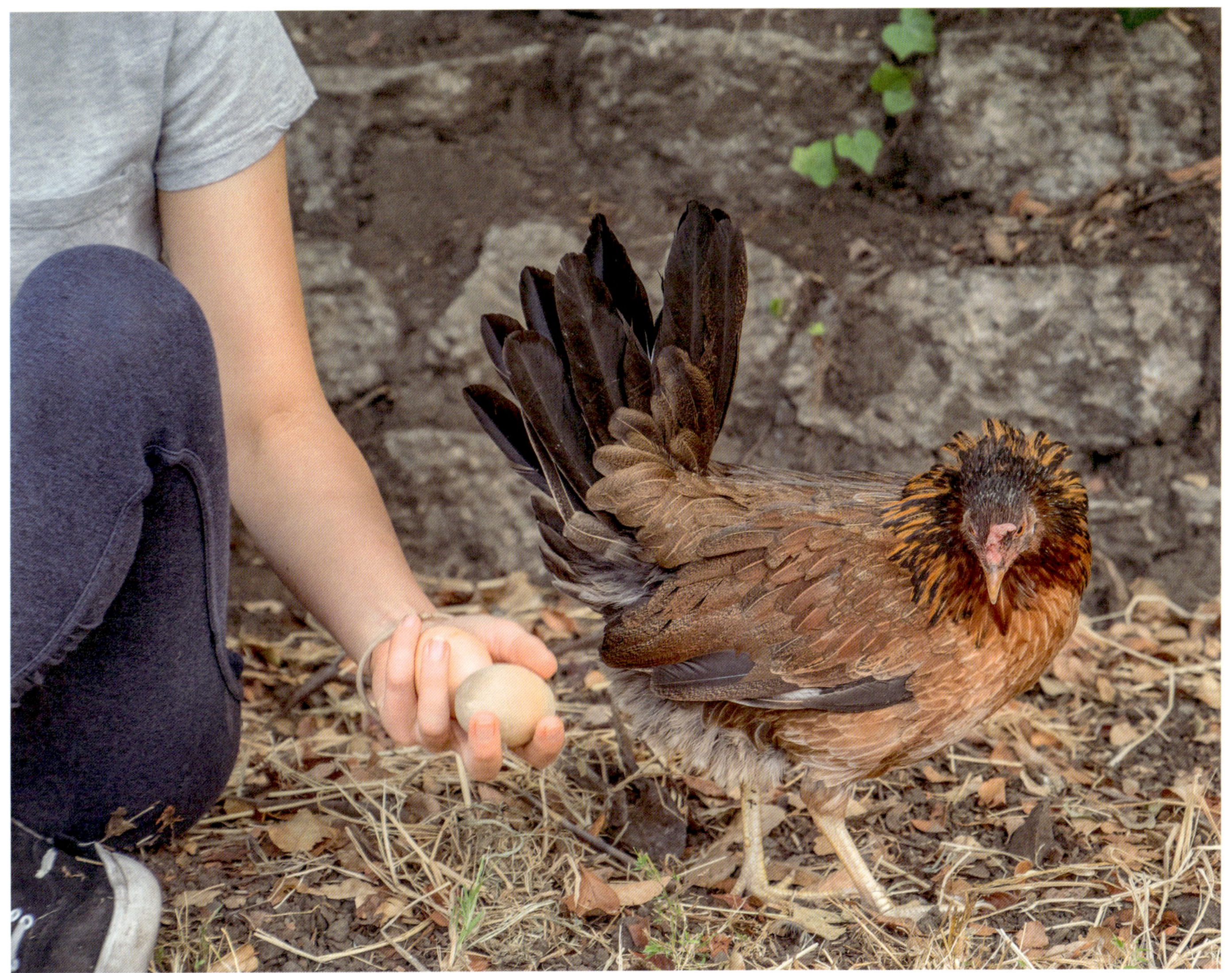

Rachel and Paprika

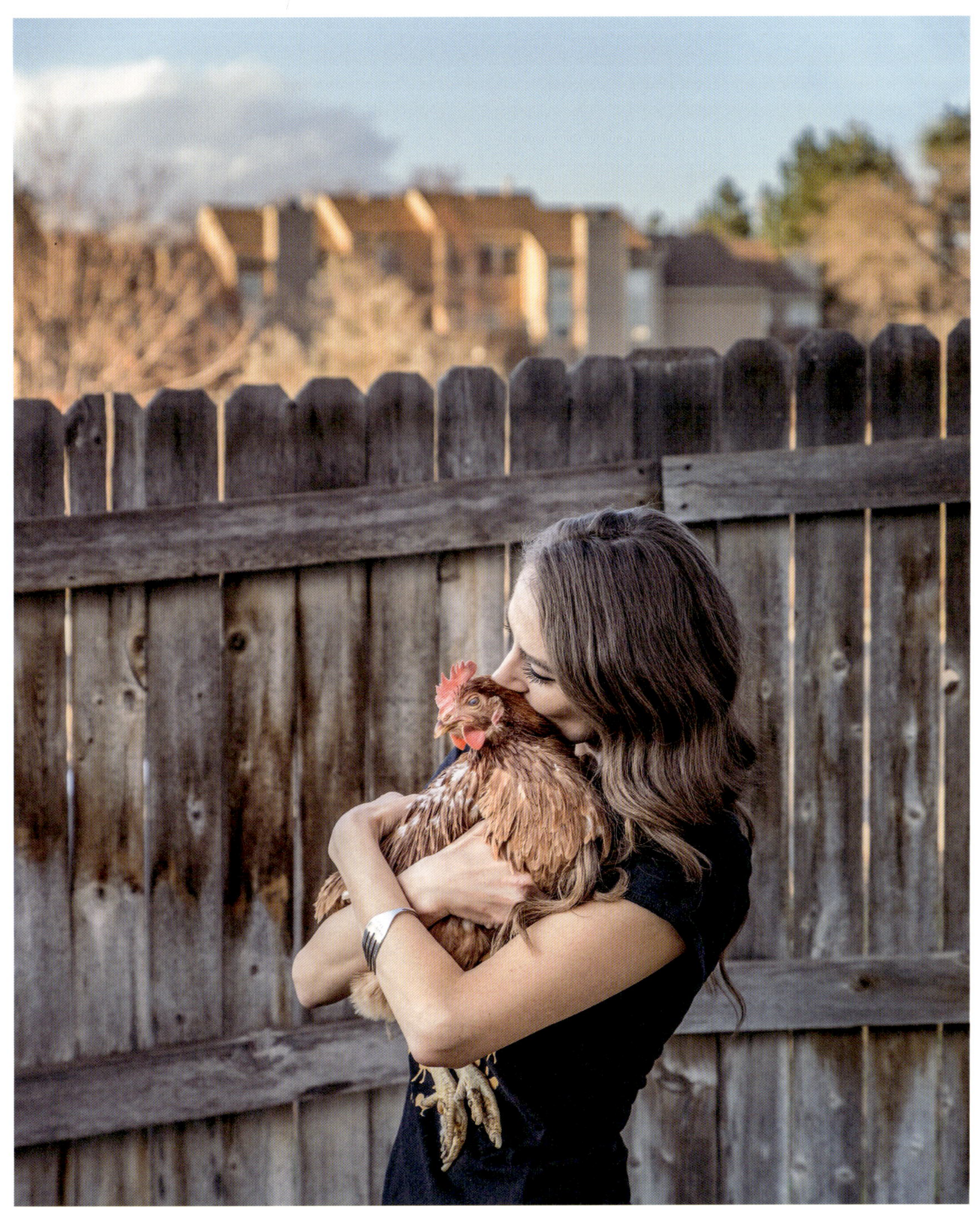

Roxanne and Kelly

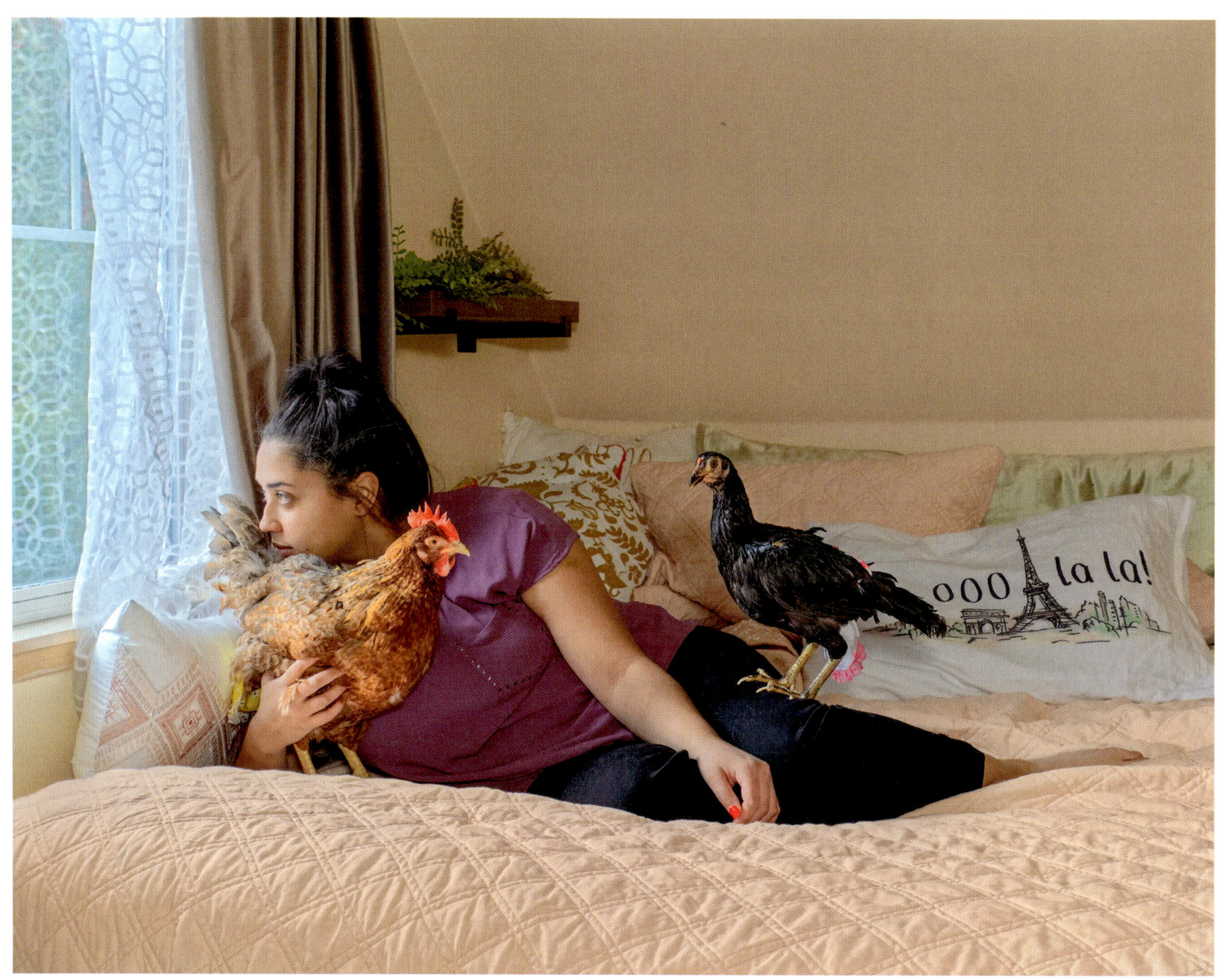

Violet, Gabrielle, and Devi

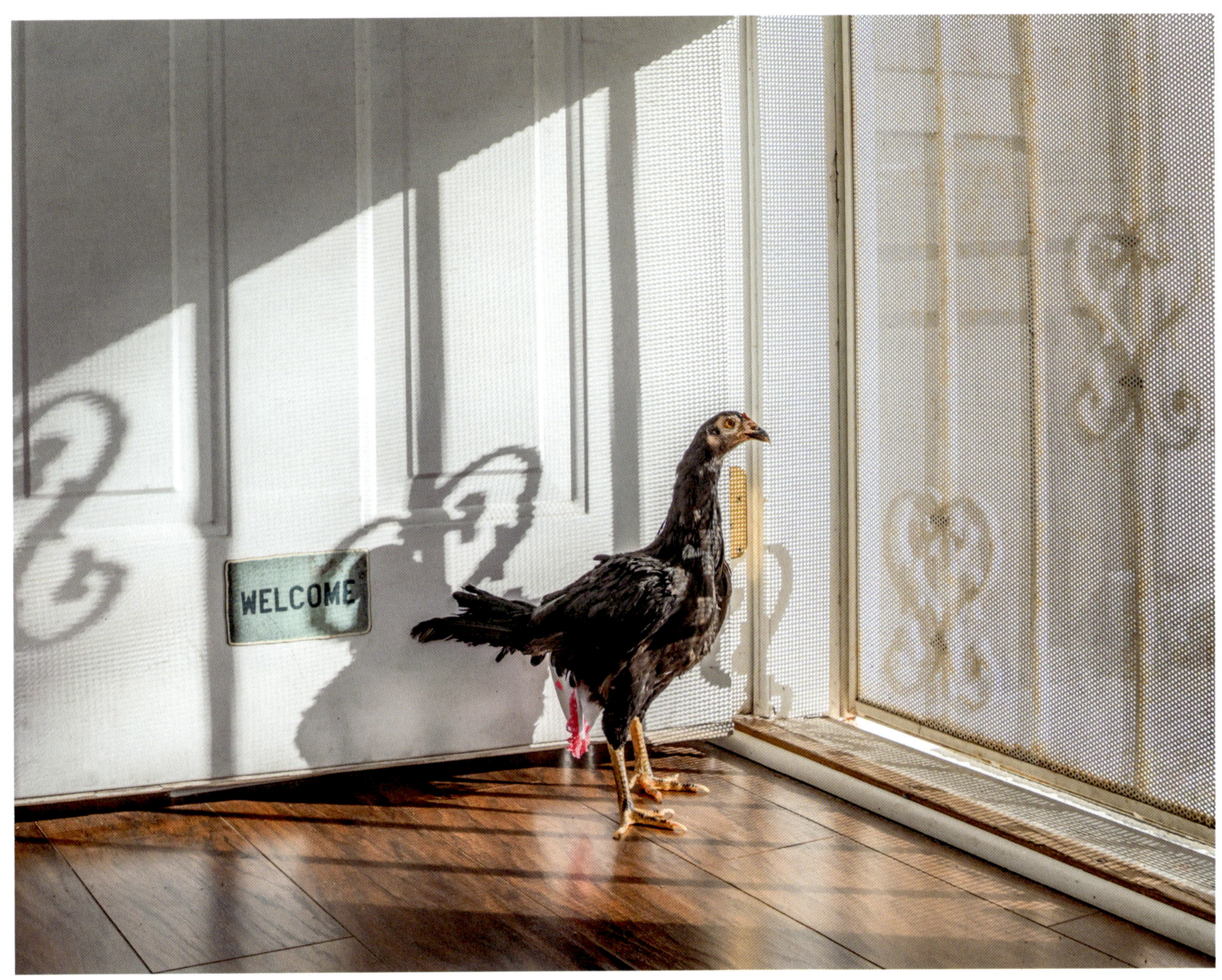

Devi

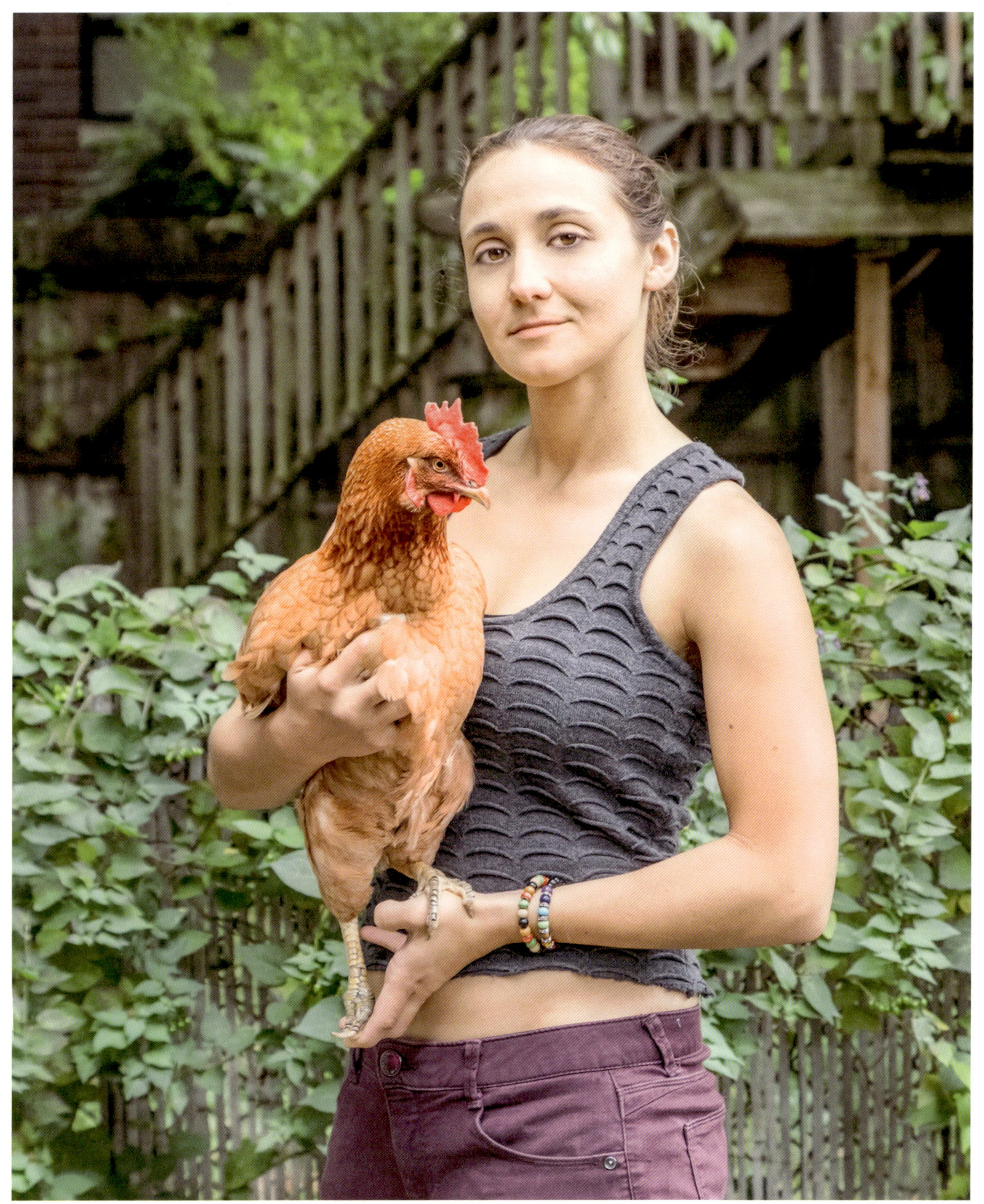

Helen and Kelsey

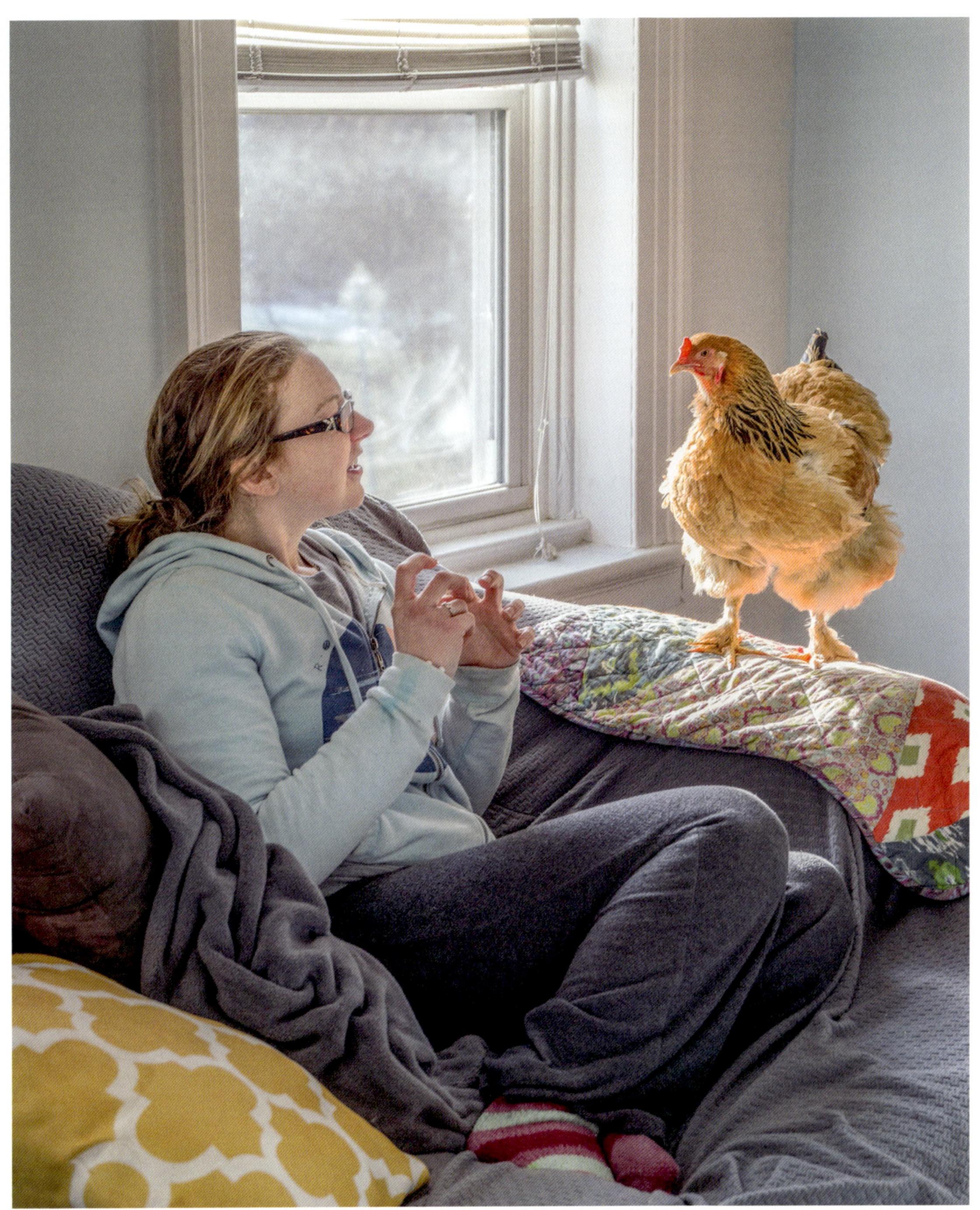

Ashley and Asa

On January 11, 2019 at 9:30 a.m. my world crashed when the vet called to tell me that my best friend, my life, my Asa, had passed away in her sleep. In her short two and a half years of life, she had struggled through many health problems including egg yolk perotonitis. The autopsy showed that her body was riddled with fast-growing, cancerous tumors.

My whole life had revolved around her, caring for and protecting her. I had quit a job I loved at an animal sanctuary so that I could earn more money to pay for her care and to buy a house where she could enjoy dustbathing in the yard.

With Asa gone, I was lost. We had a routine and I didn't know what to do without her. At first, I couldn't even sleep in my room because she wasn't there with me like she should have been. I blamed myself, thinking obsessively about what I might have done differently to help her. I kept myself surrounded by her things. I wasn't ready to pack them away.

Asa should still be here, jumping on my shoulder, preening my hair at night to tell me she is ready for bed, cuddling close to my heart when we're lying together, waking me up in the morning to ask for breakfast. If I listen carefully, I can still hear her contented purring.

She was the most loved person, my everything. I still have my days when I break down but I am slowly getting better. I know that I did everything I could to help her. As much as my heart hurts and I know that I will never fully heal, in honor of my best friend I am going to stay strong and continue to rescue those in need. Every farmed animal deserves to experience love just like my Asa did. My feather-footed, tiny dinosaur queen. I miss you so much every day.

Ashley Snyder

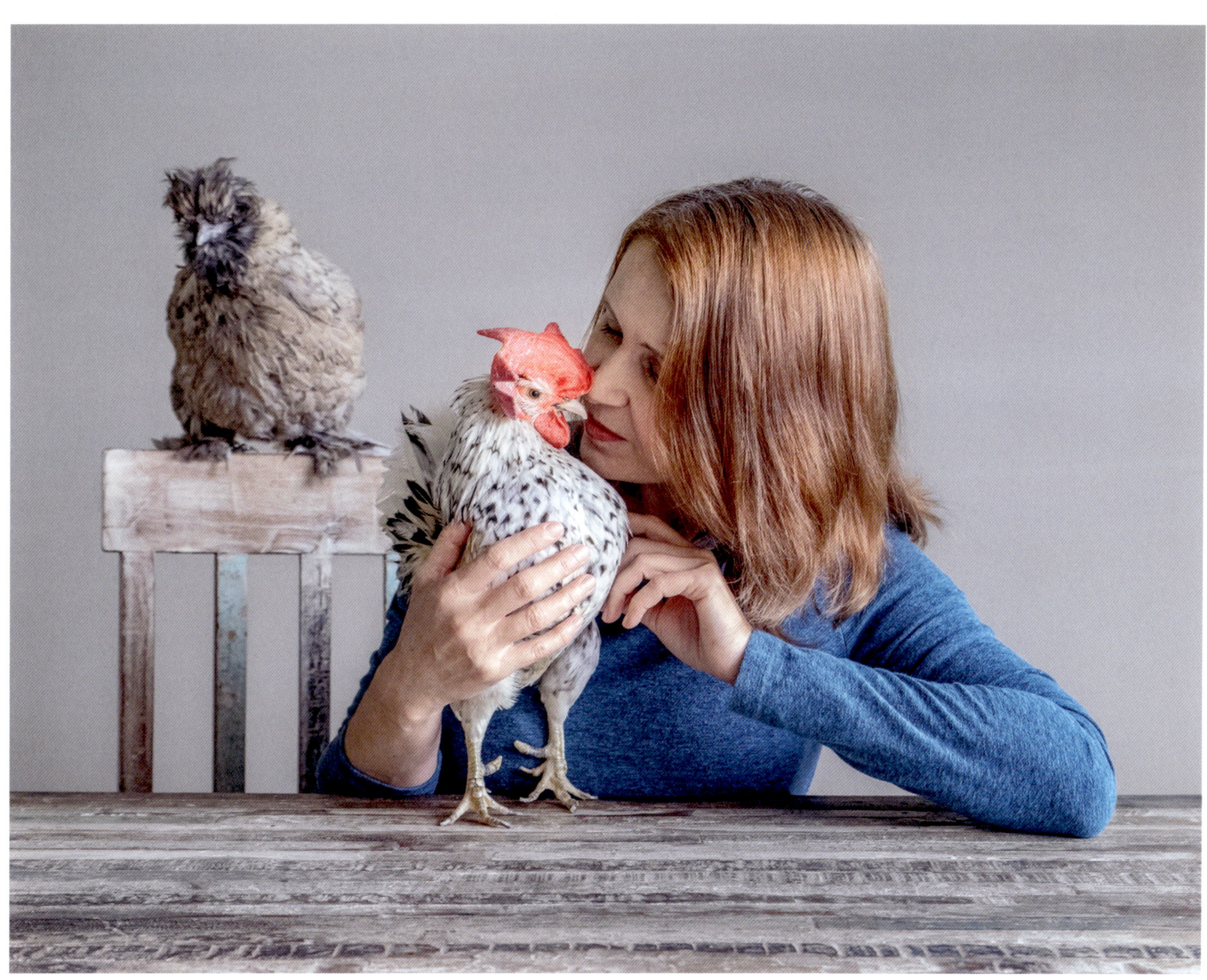

Serena, Yetti, and Kasia

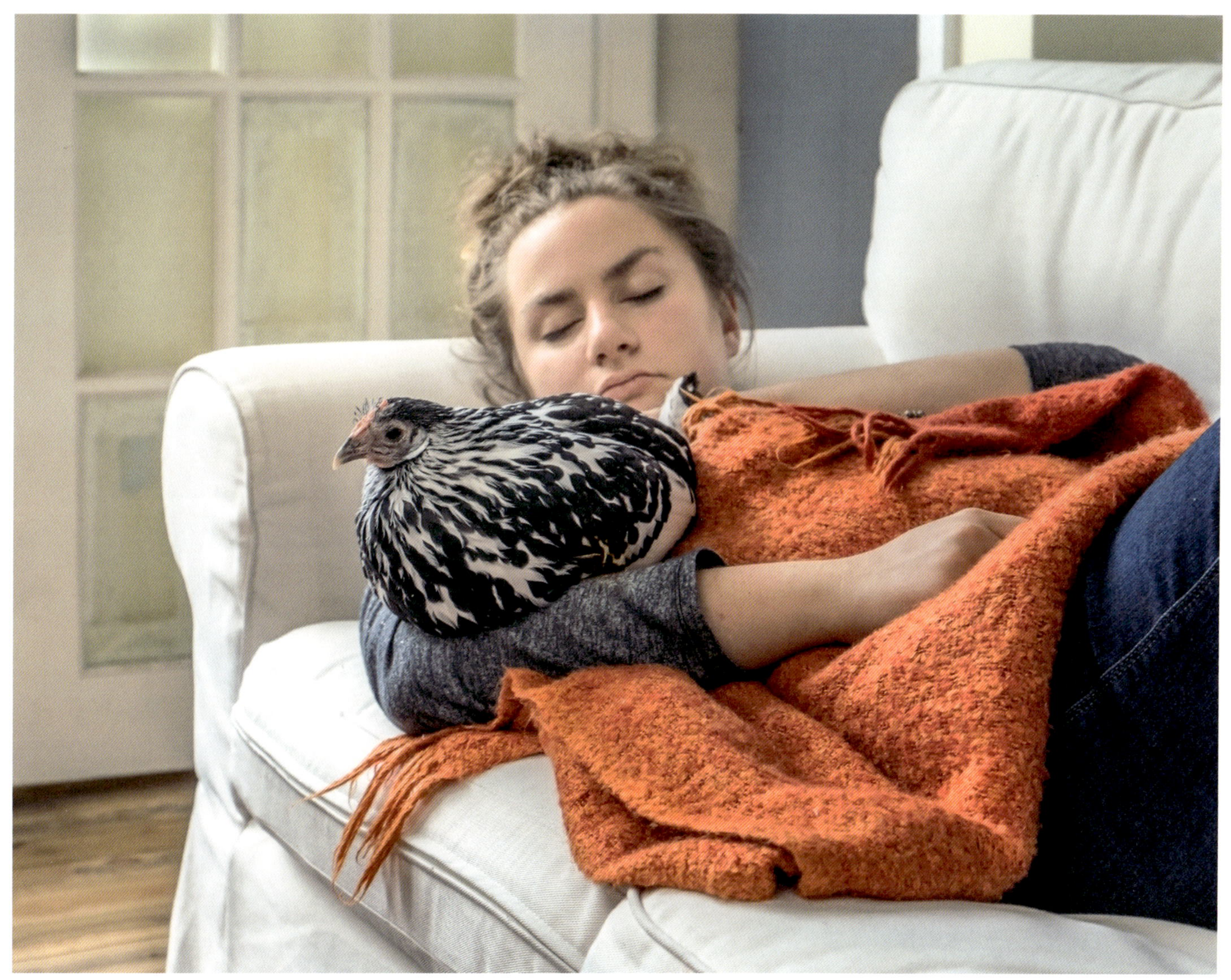

Josie and Rachel

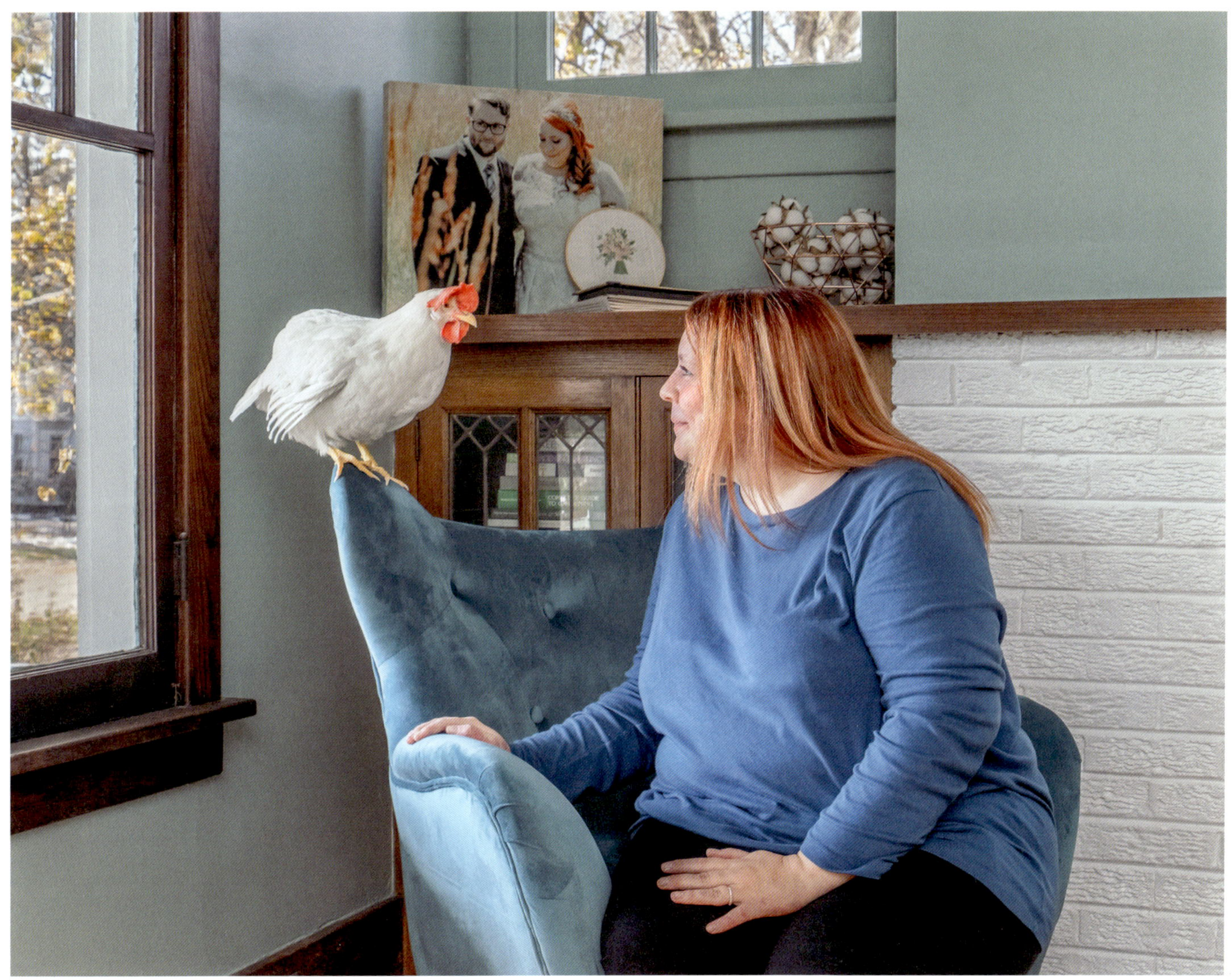

Winnie and April

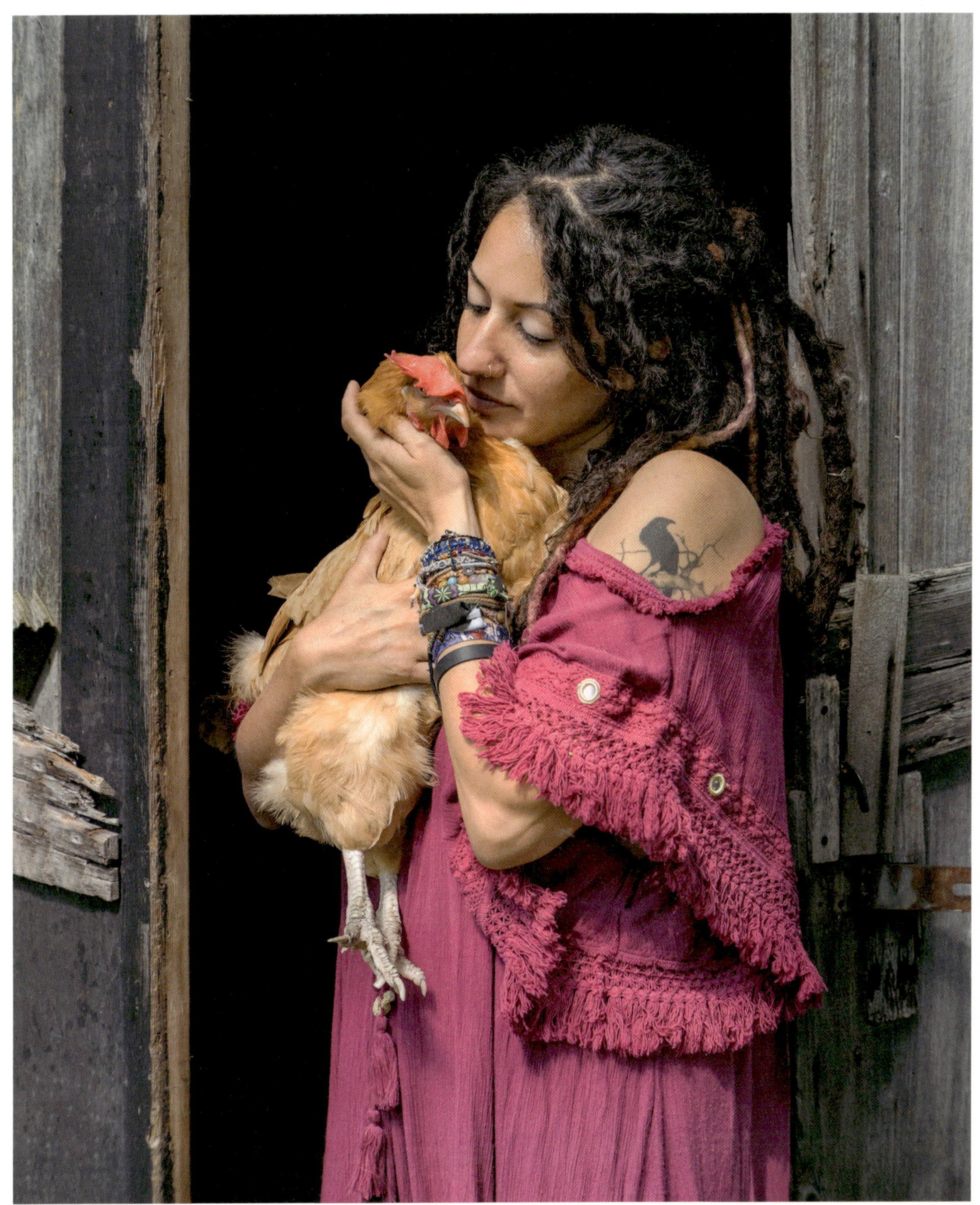

Valencia Jayne and Rehana

And what about the roosters born to laying hens? Unneeded and unloved, many are killed shortly after birth, often by being suffocated, crushed, or ground up alive. Others are abandoned or killed as soon as they start crowing. Local laws that permit backyard hens but prohibit roosters exacerbate the problem.

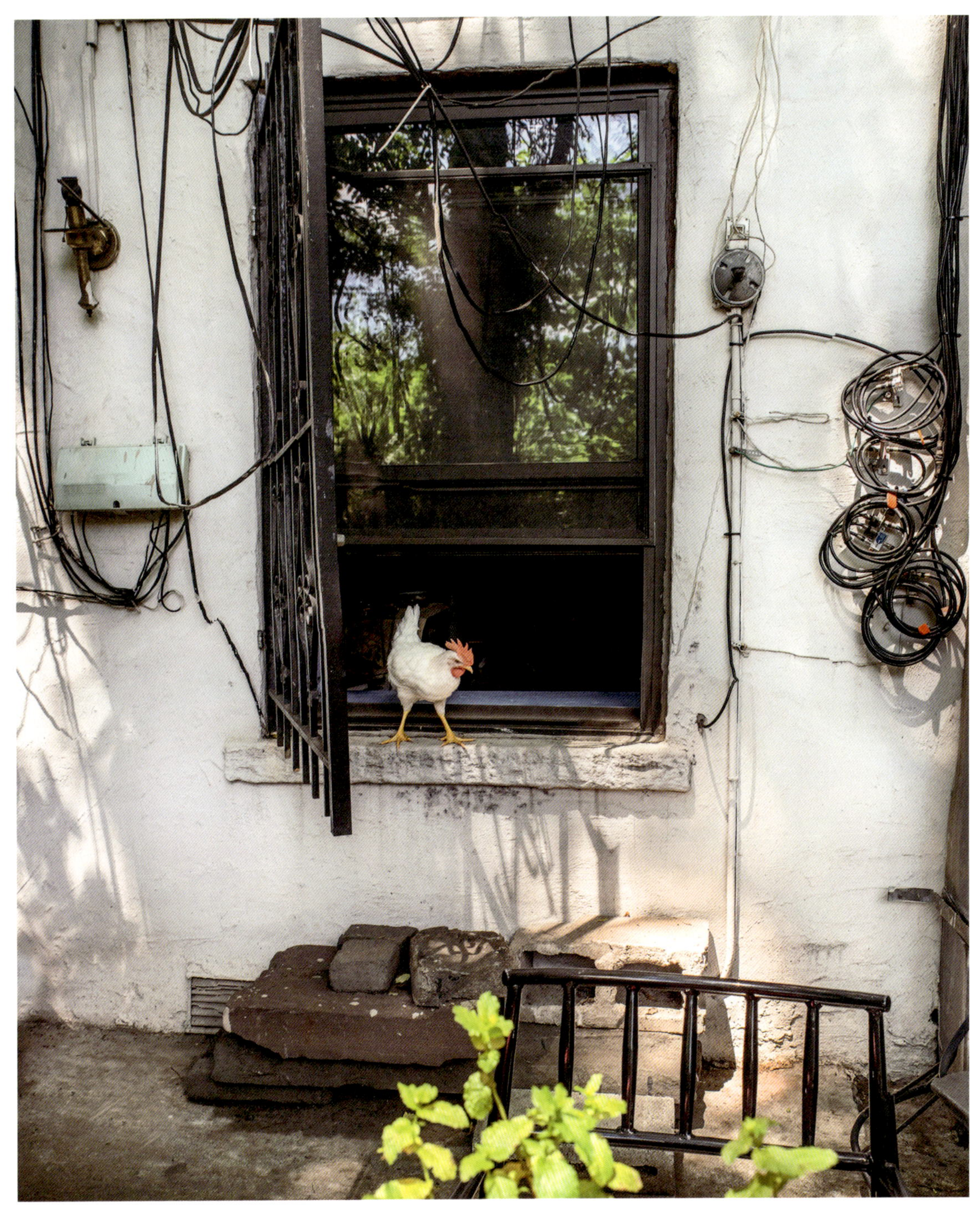

Bree

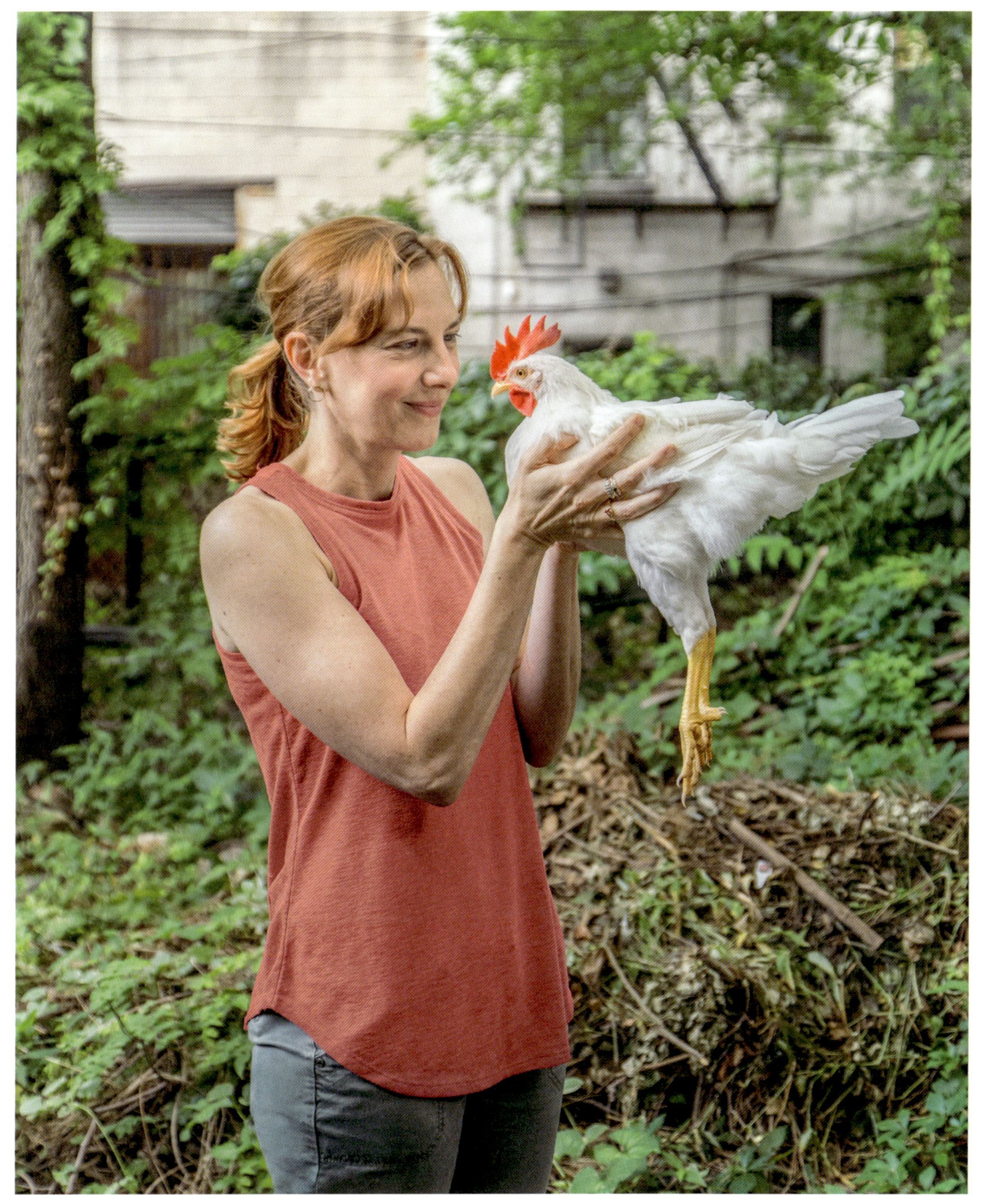

Camille and Bree

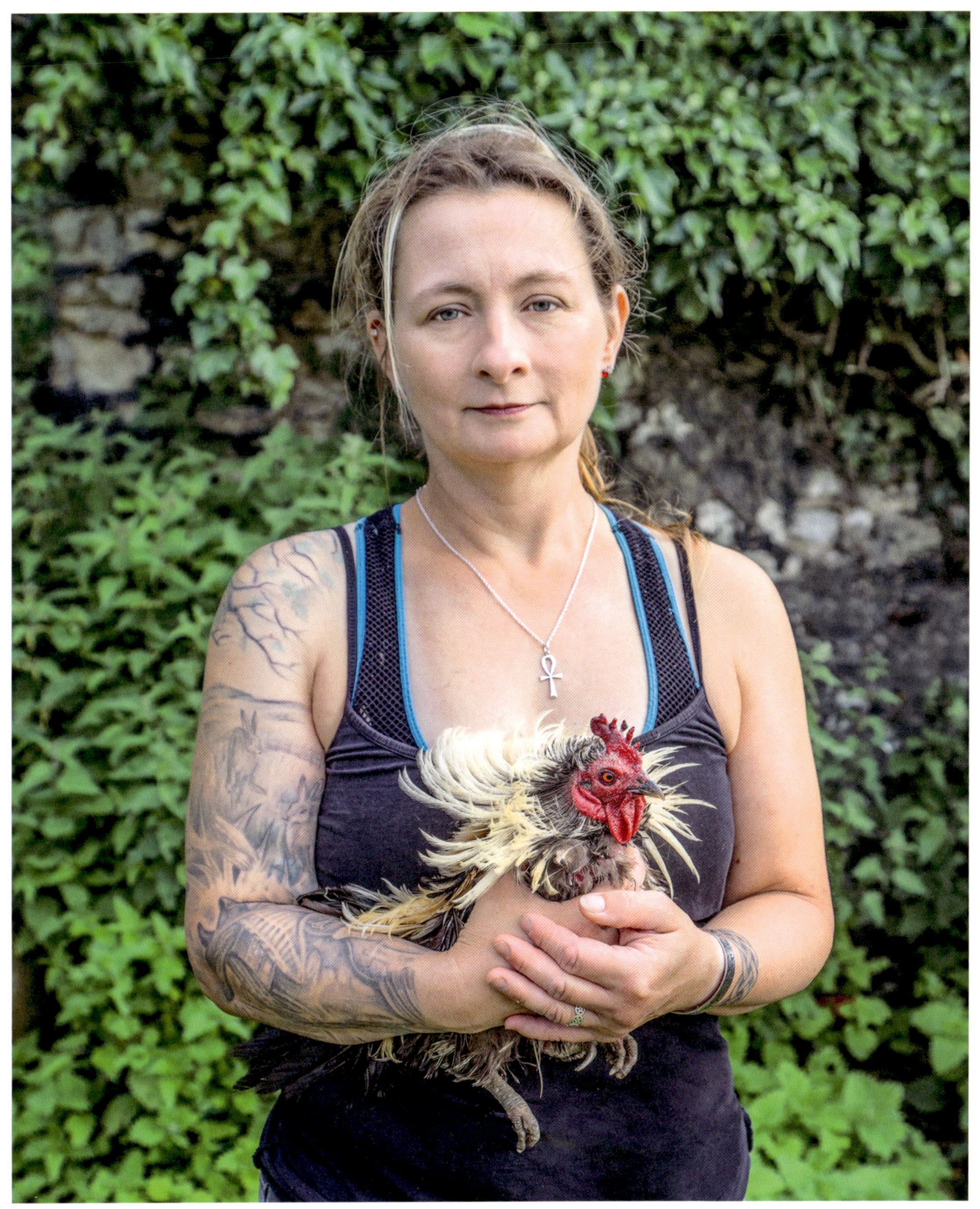

Mel and Harold

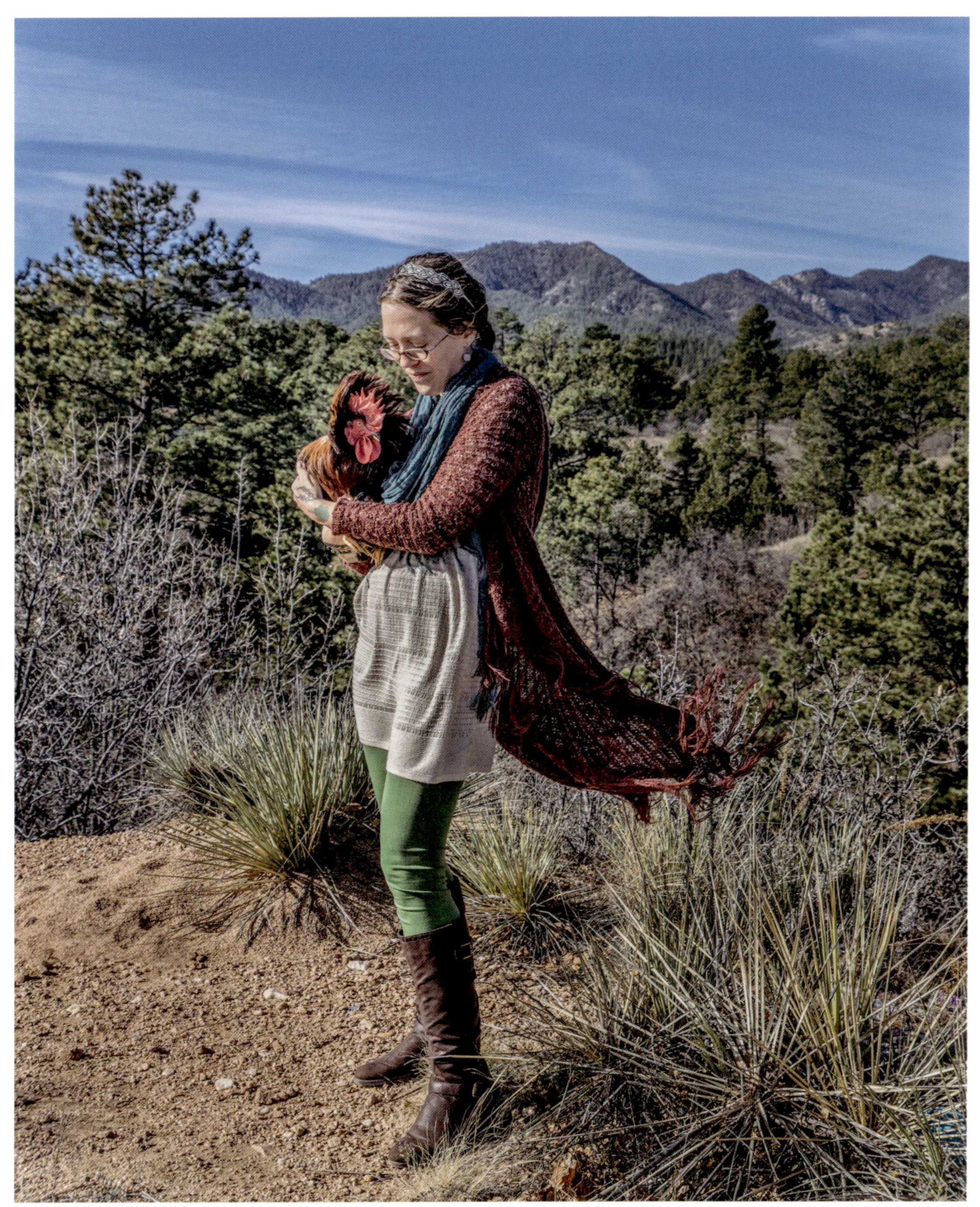

G.Lee and Jade

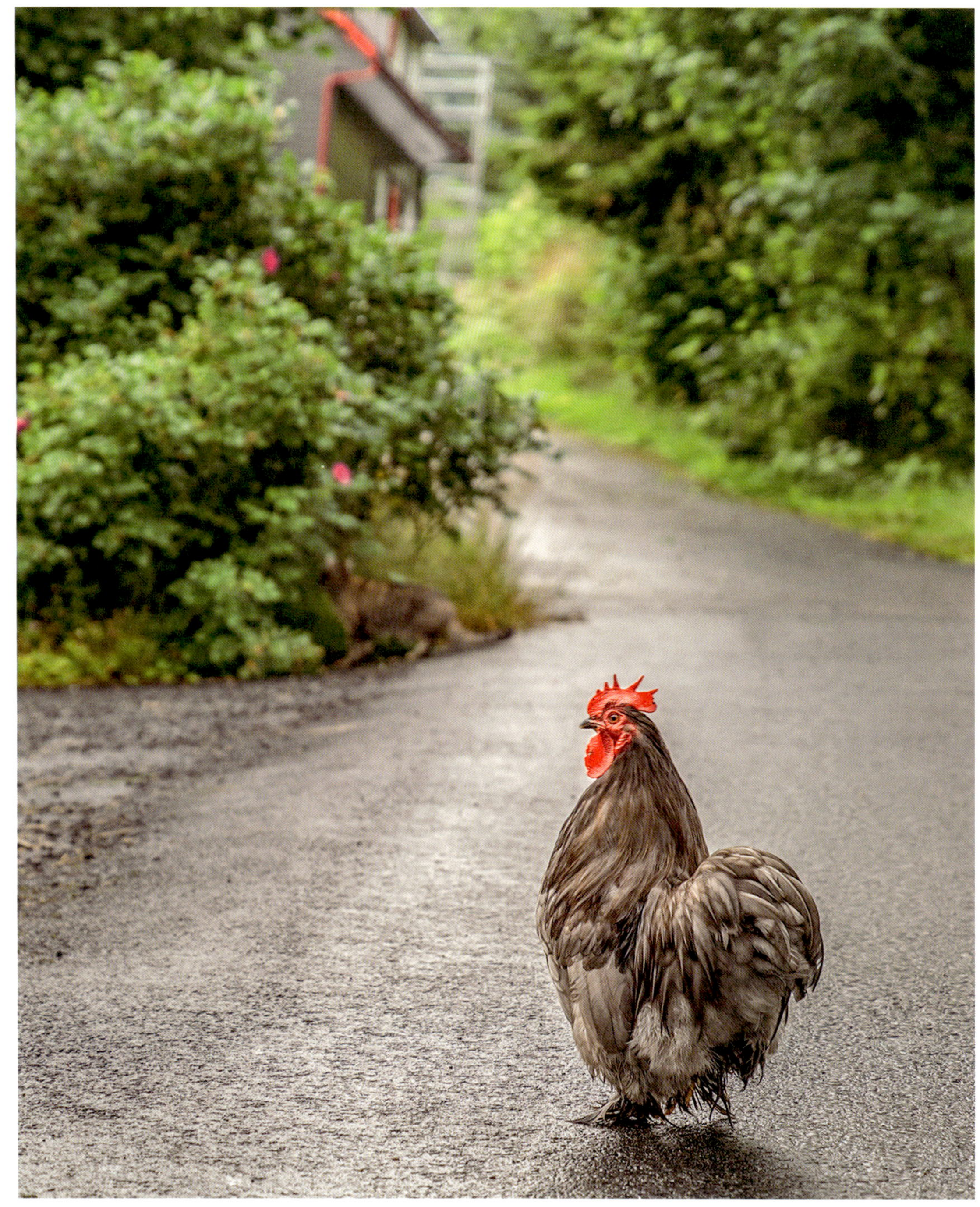

Dog

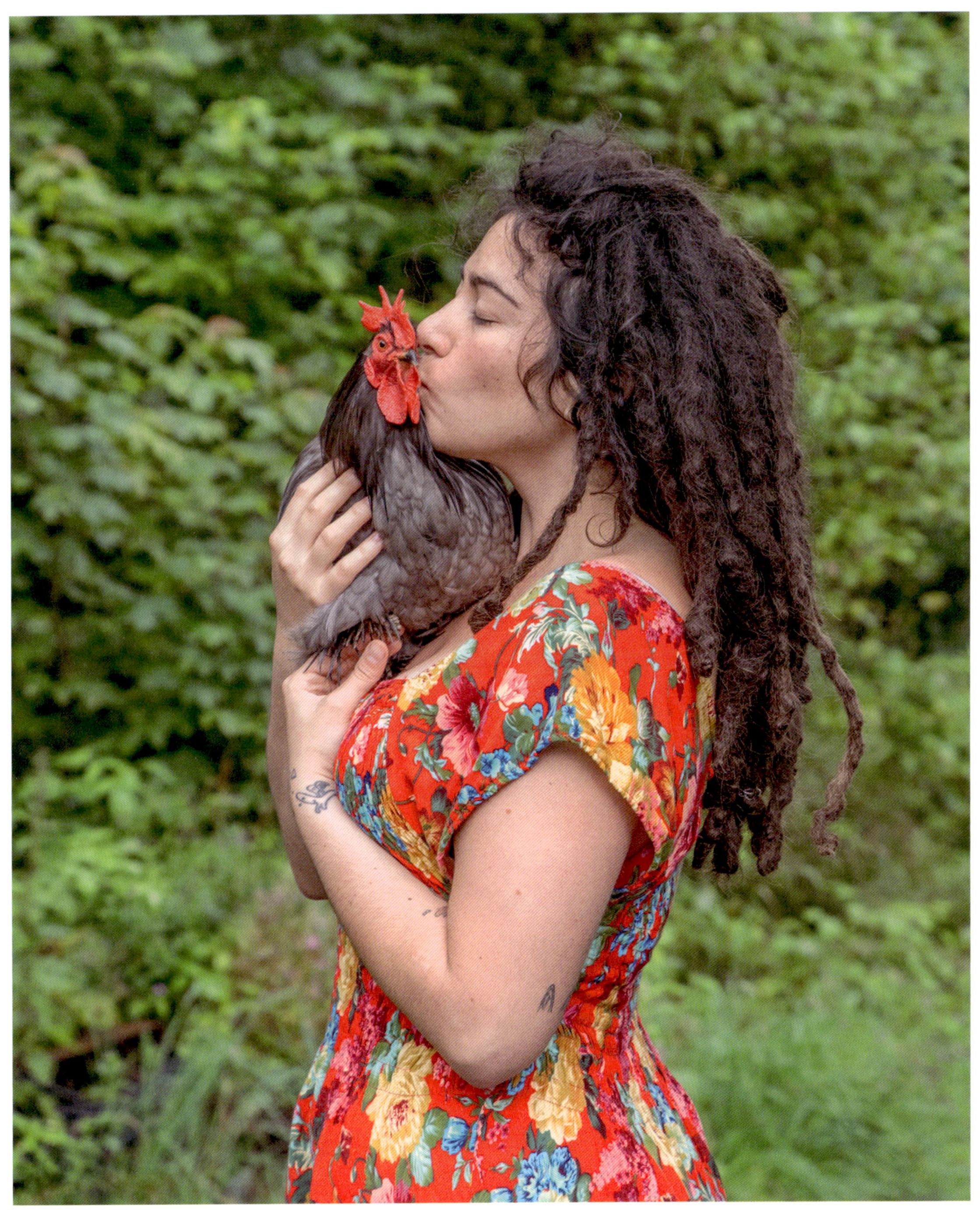

Dog and Elaine

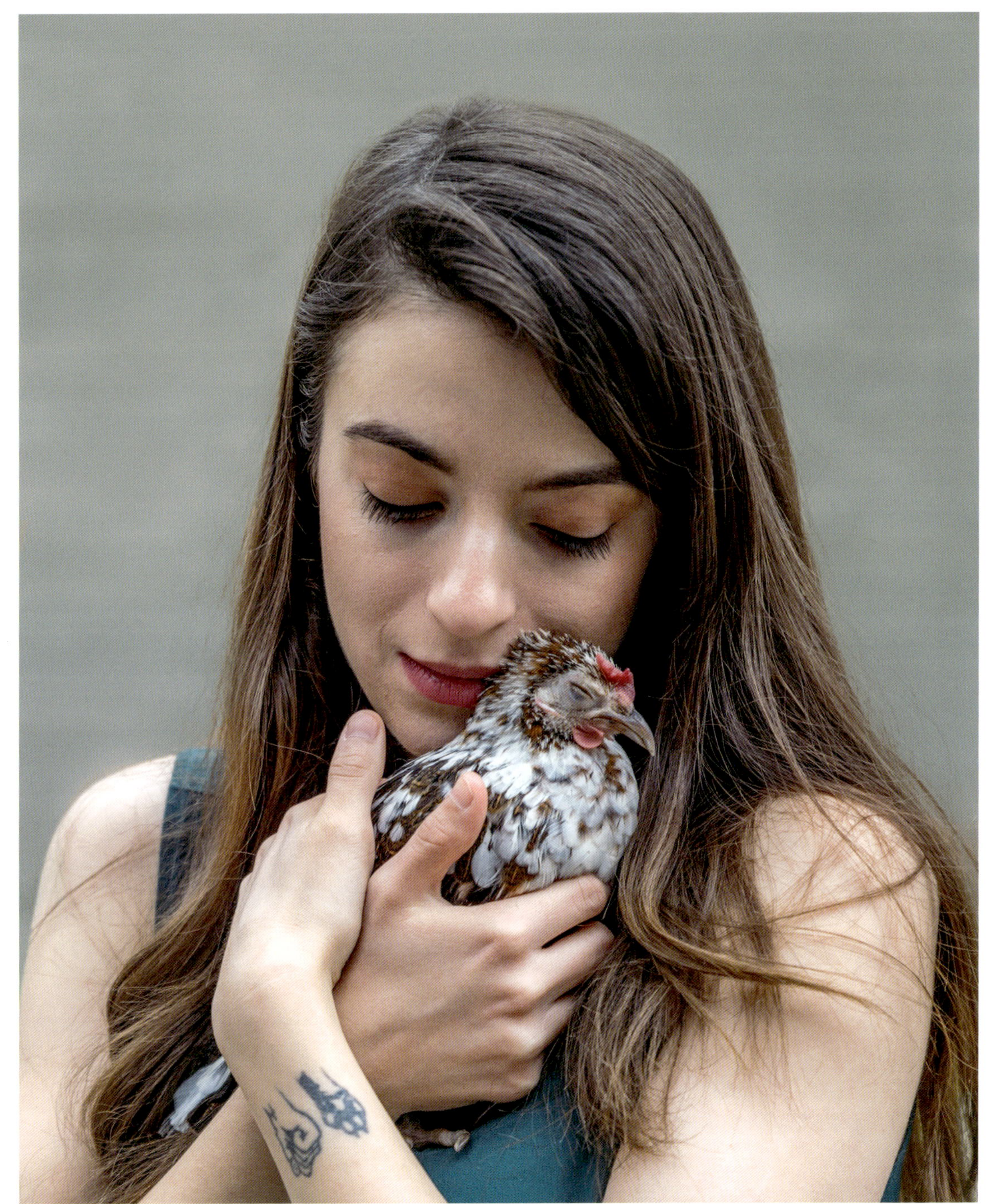

Rocky and Eloise

After a long battle with a chronic, incurable, and ultimately fatal virus, Eloise died in my arms.

Eloise was a presence, which makes her absence all the more painful. She loved fiercely, communicated clearly, complained loudly, hated wholeheartedly, and trusted implicitly. From flying great distances to snuggle with me, yelling until I opened a door, or resting in the collar of my sweater, there wasn't a single moment when she failed to make her feelings under-stood. And so when she felt unwell, although she persevered, this, too, I understood loud and clear.

She was my friend, my companion, my charge, my equal, my family. Losing her felt nothing short of losing my own blood.

Nothing compares to what she experienced, but there is a particular agony to being someone's guardian and caregiver, and trying so hard to keep them well, only to face an inevitable crushing loss. Her illness was respiratory. She strained to simply breathe. And so I spent hours upon hours clearing out her throat, scraping away plaques, trying to help her find air. For many months, keeping Eloise alive was the reason I lived. And

when someone becomes the center of your world so completely, it can be hard to know how to continue without them.
There were times when I felt convinced I couldn't. There are
times now when her death compounds with those of all my
other friends who I've watched die and I feel physically crushed
by the weight, unable to move. Grief can feel unbearable and it
never truly goes away.

The world has been darker without Eloise in it. She took a piece
of me with her, but it's a piece I'll never regret giving. I will
forever love this little bird with all my heart.

————————————

Rocky Schwartz

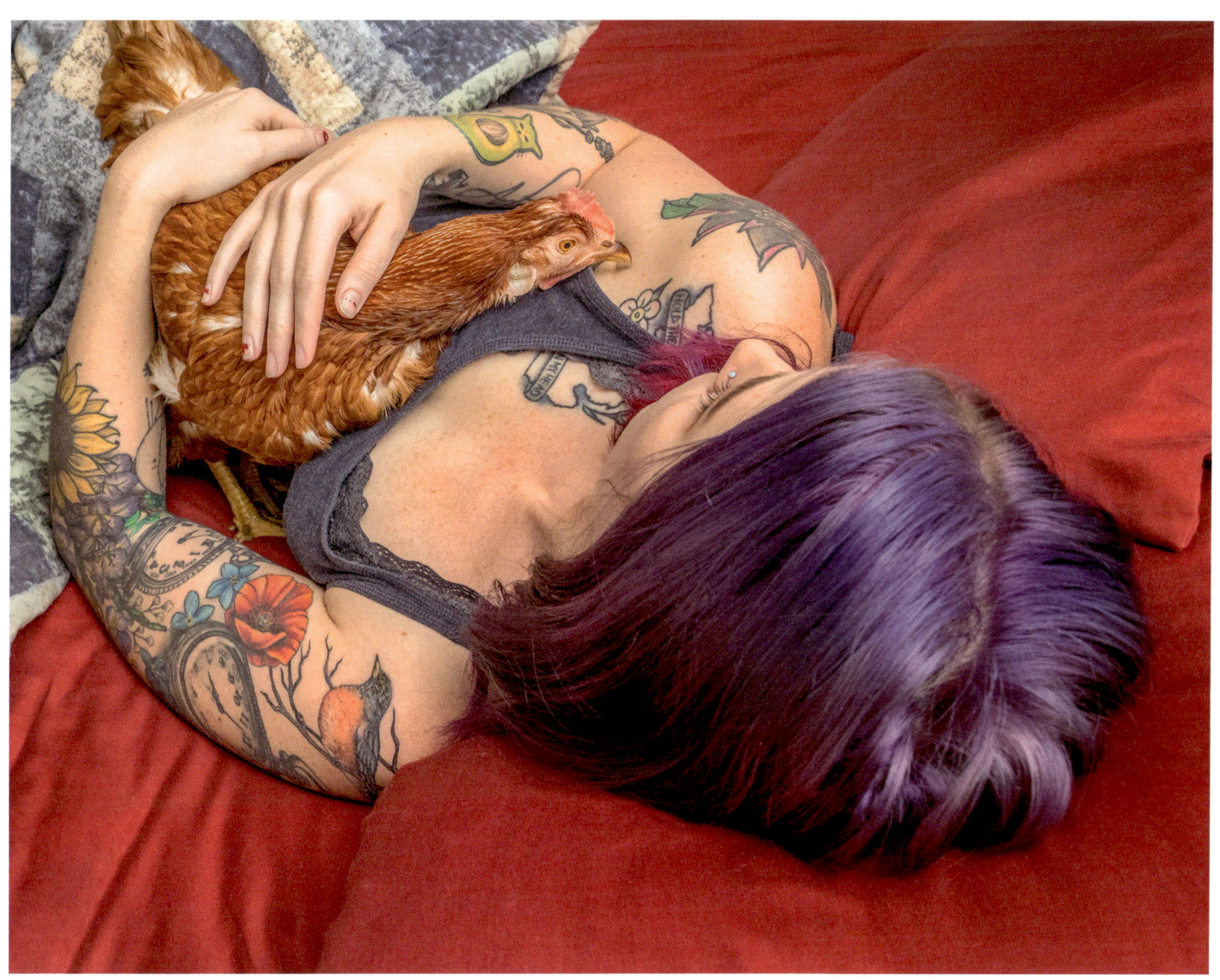

Marsha and Nikki

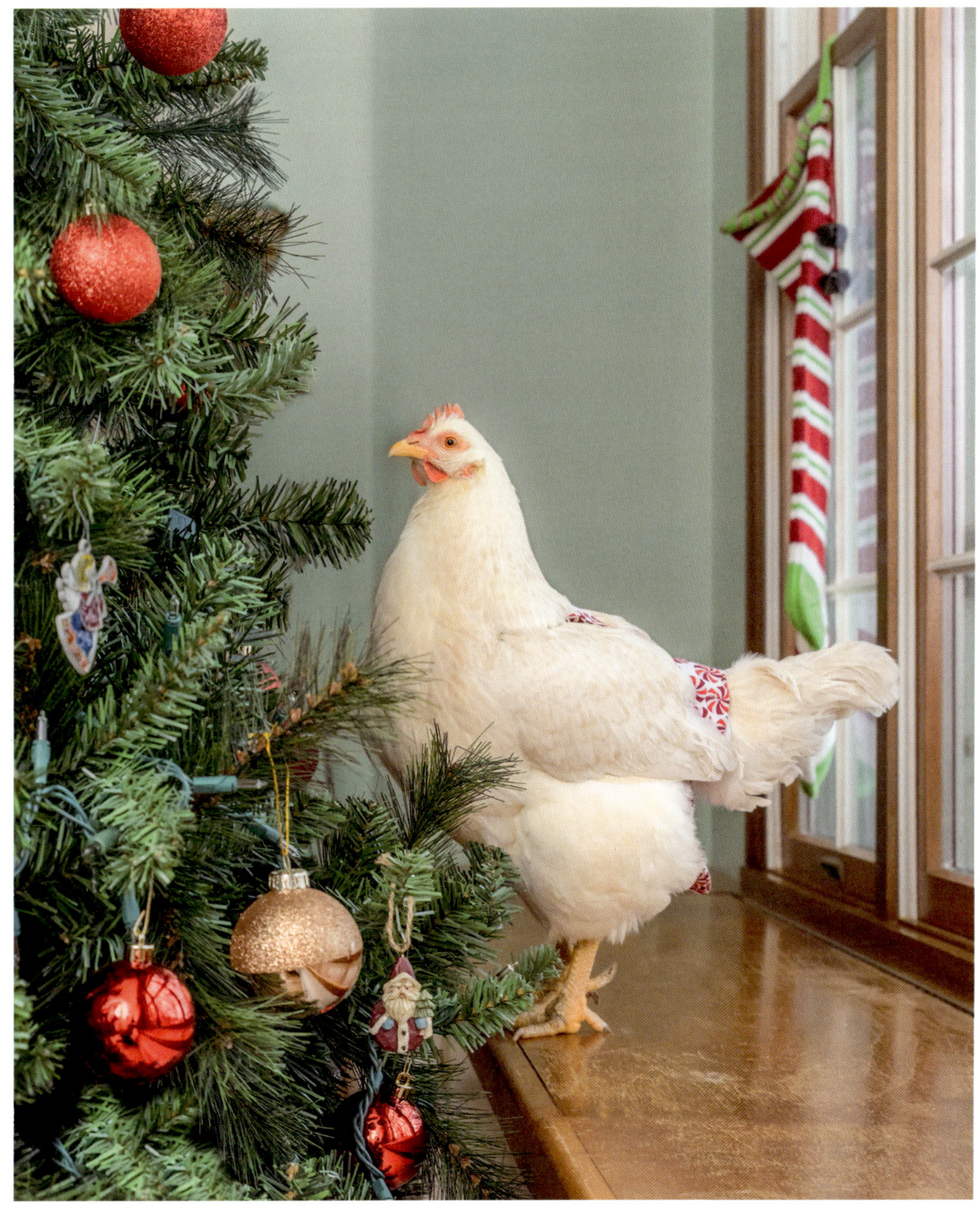

Gloria

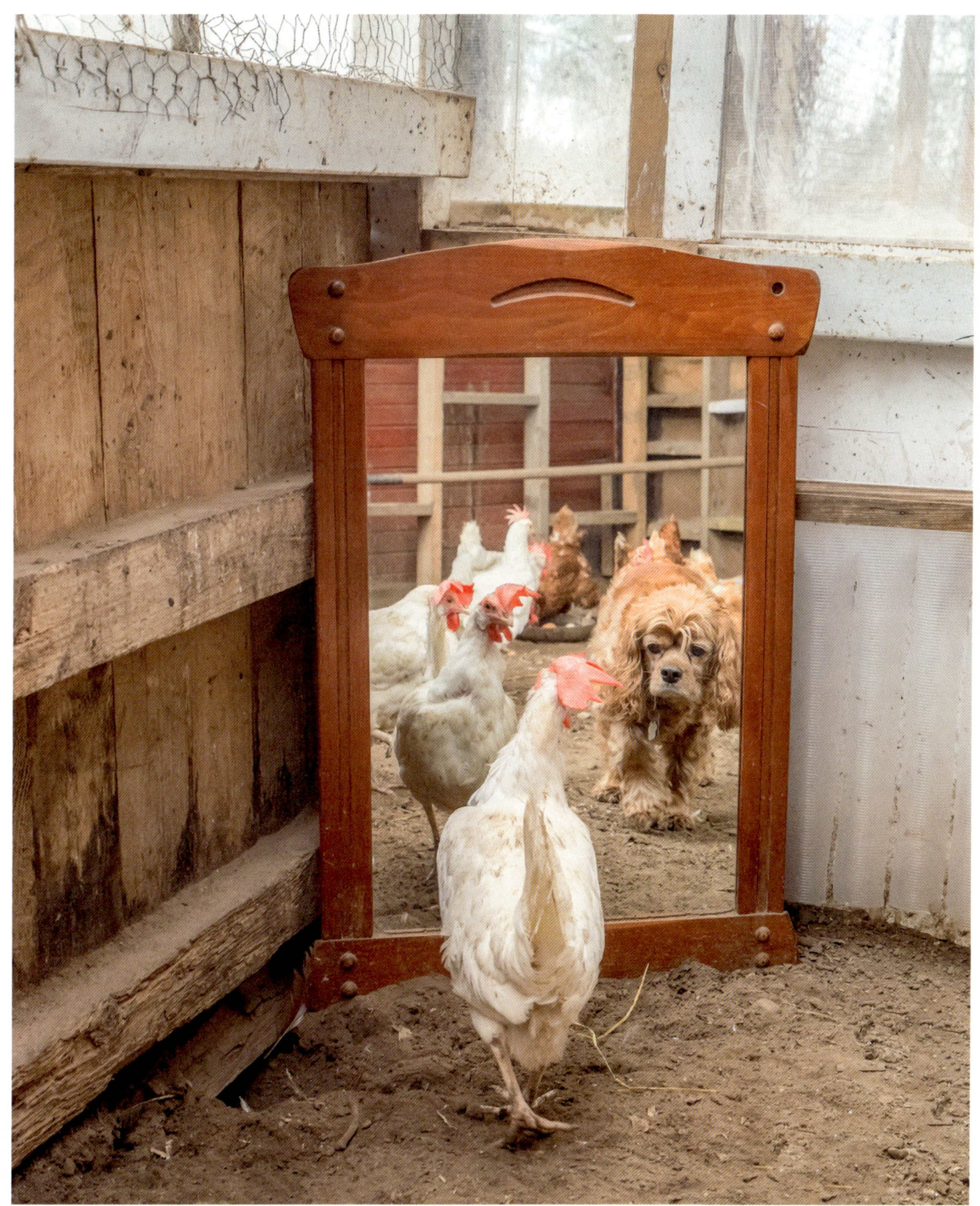

Cissie and Casey

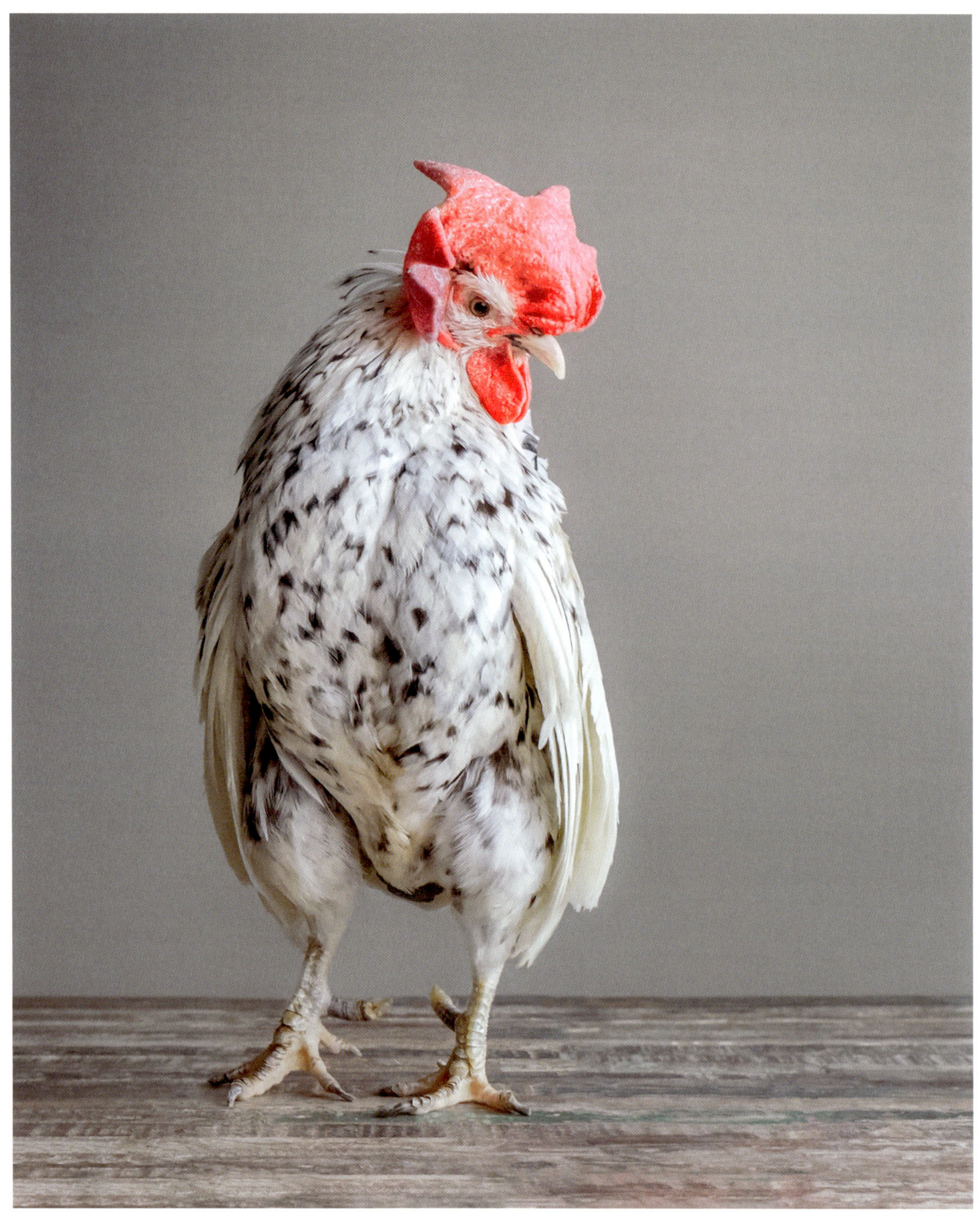

Yetti

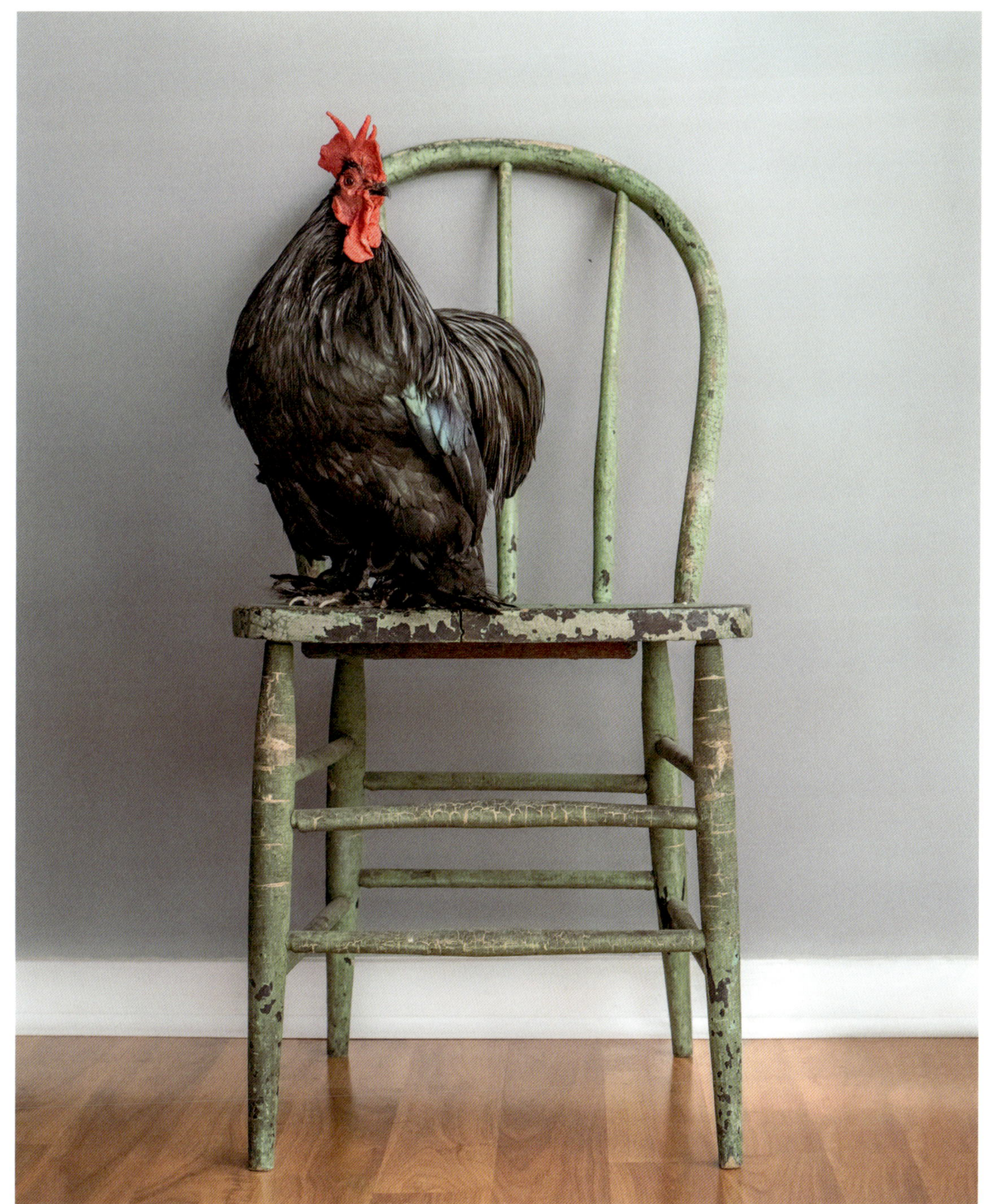

Tonto

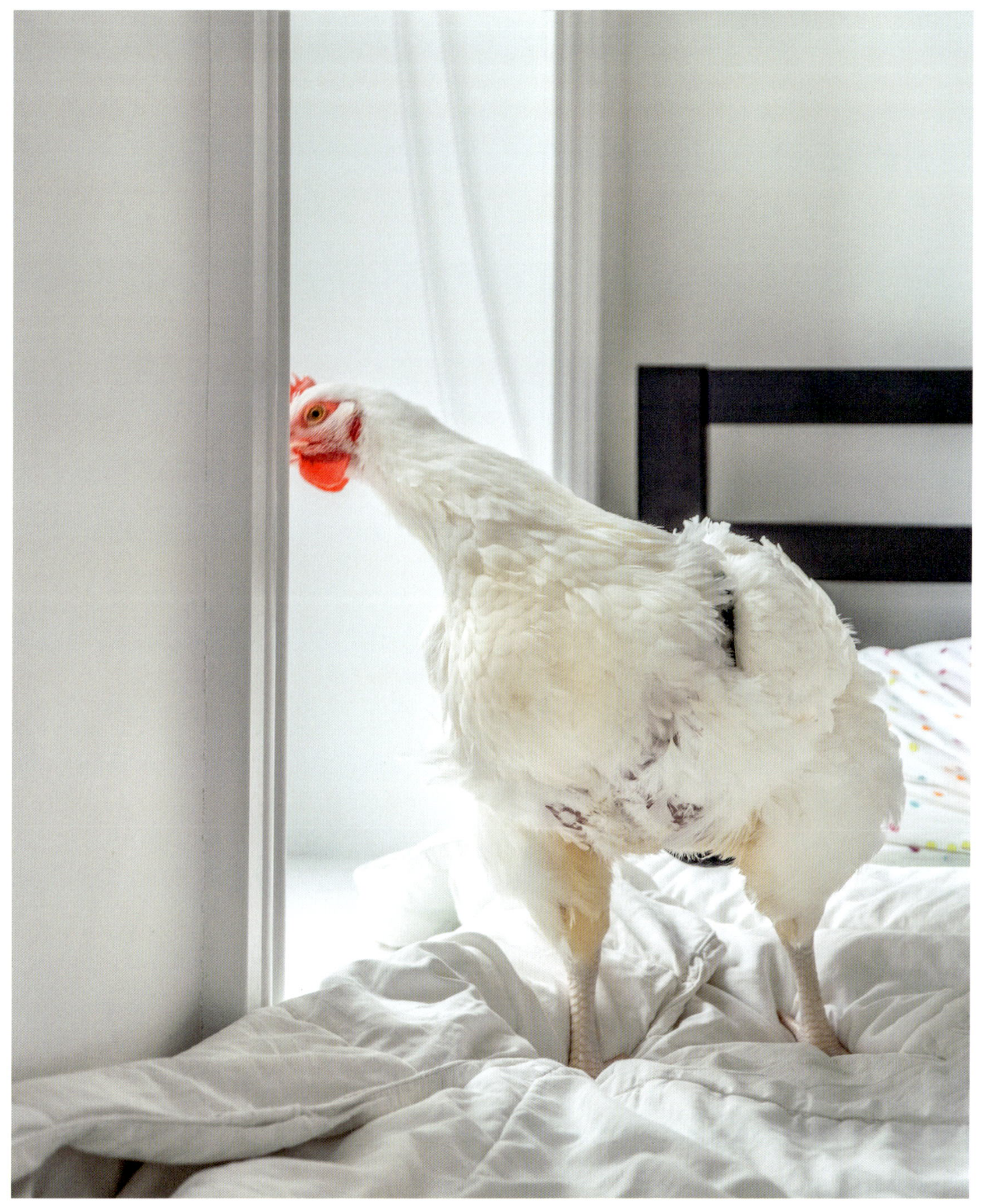

Rose

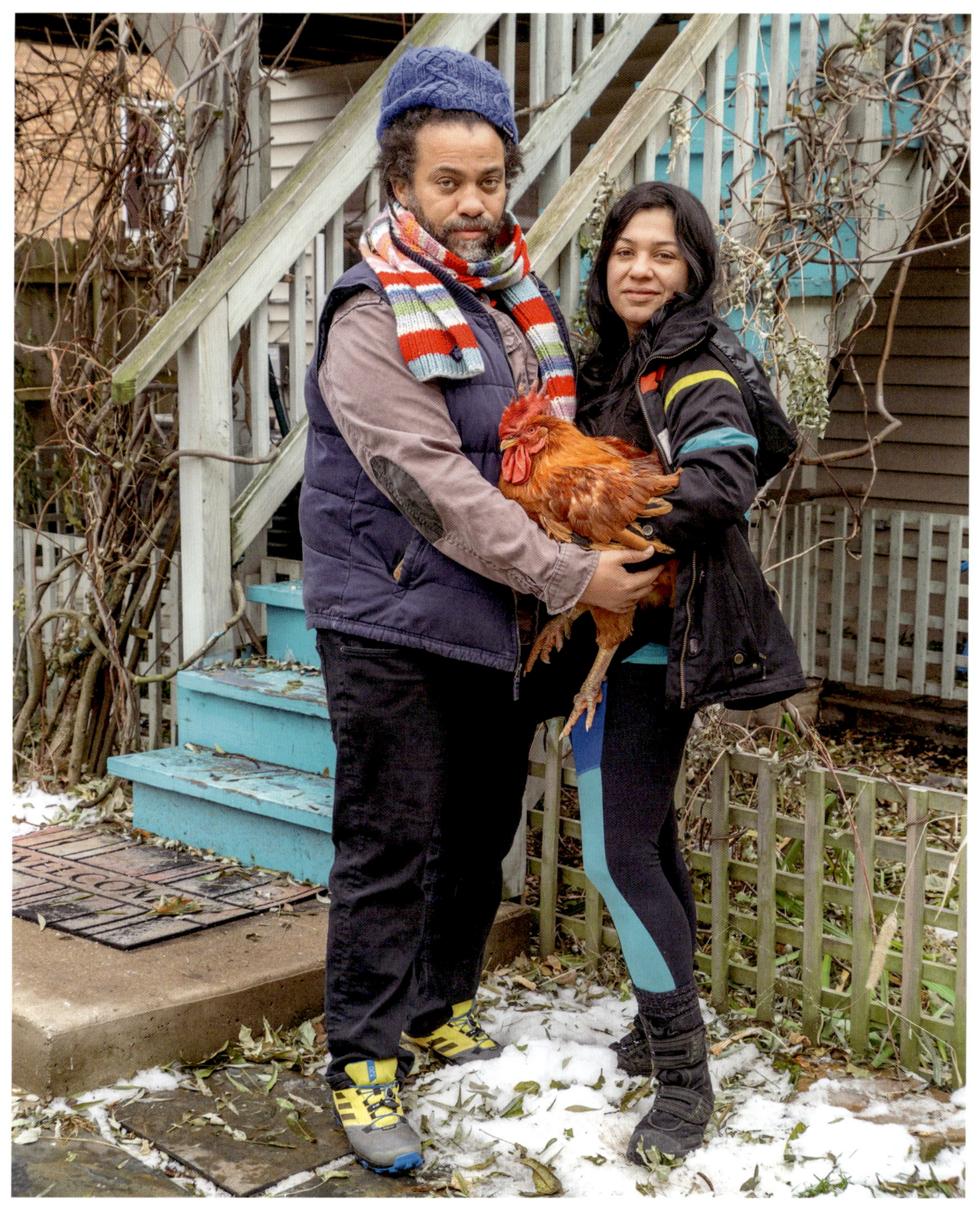

Cosmos, Leonard Crowen, and Julia

On my fortieth birthday I ran into a room full of shrieking, trau-matized birds. The night before, Chicago Animal Care and Con-trol had seized 114 chickens from a cockfighting ring and then driven them straight to our friends at Chicago Chicken Rescue. They took as many as they could.

The screams of remaining birds who landed at CACC echoed off the walls. The roosters' combs and wattles had been cut off. Their spurs were chopped for easy placement of metal spurs. Their breasts were red, raw, bruised, and cut. All for the sake of human entertainment.

At first I thought we would have to pick who would live or die because it would be very difficult to find homes for them, espe-cially for the roosters. But Quincy from Farm Bird Sanctuary joined us that morning and quickly others joined us. Our com-munity coalesced as the Chicago Roo Crew, committed to healing and finding homes for as many birds as we could.

As our friends and allies transferred the hens, chicks, and the most critically ill birds to sanctuaries and vets, the Roo Crew began putting our hands on each and every rooster. We gave them pain medication. We wrapped their poor, infected feet. We treated them for mites and respiratory infections. We did our best. We kept on doing our best.

No one thought that all 114 birds could be saved. But they were. Every single rooster, hen, and chick got a chance at life in sanctuary and freedom, and most of them are still alive with us. Loving people in ten states opened their hearts, homes, and sanctuaries. Many of the people who stood up for those birds were women and people of color. The last eleven roosters were adopted by a Latinx family with experience rescuing injured and dying birds from cockfighting pits. Their kindness melted us.

The Chicago Roo Crew is proud of what we have done as female leaders in our community. We embrace the world's most exploited land animal. We stand strong, defying and rejecting the stereotypes projected on people of color when it comes to animal abuse. We know that we are at our best together.

And we are with them, the non-human animals with whom we share this planet. We always will be.

———————

Julia Magnus

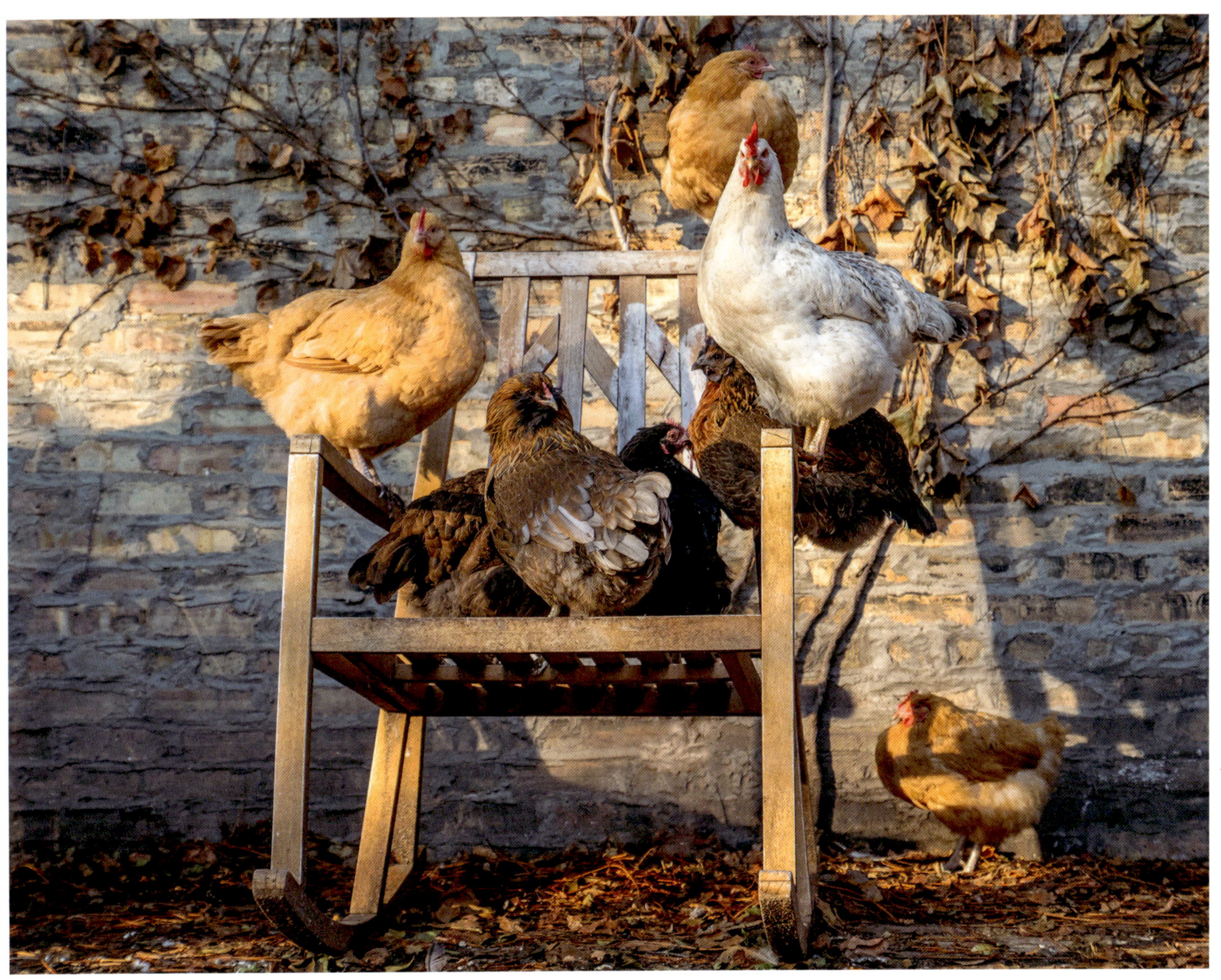

Chicago Chicken Rescue

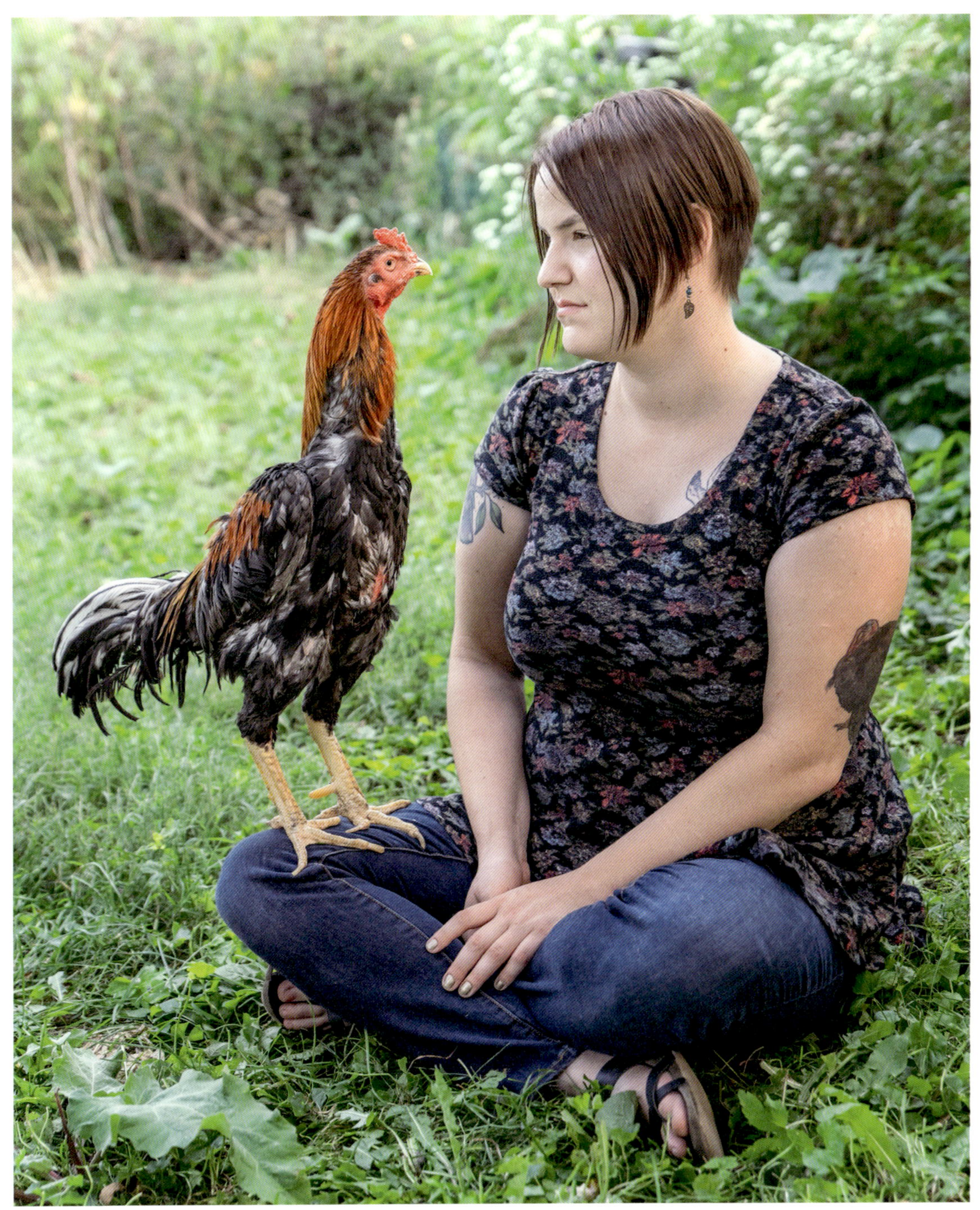

Reuben and Quincy

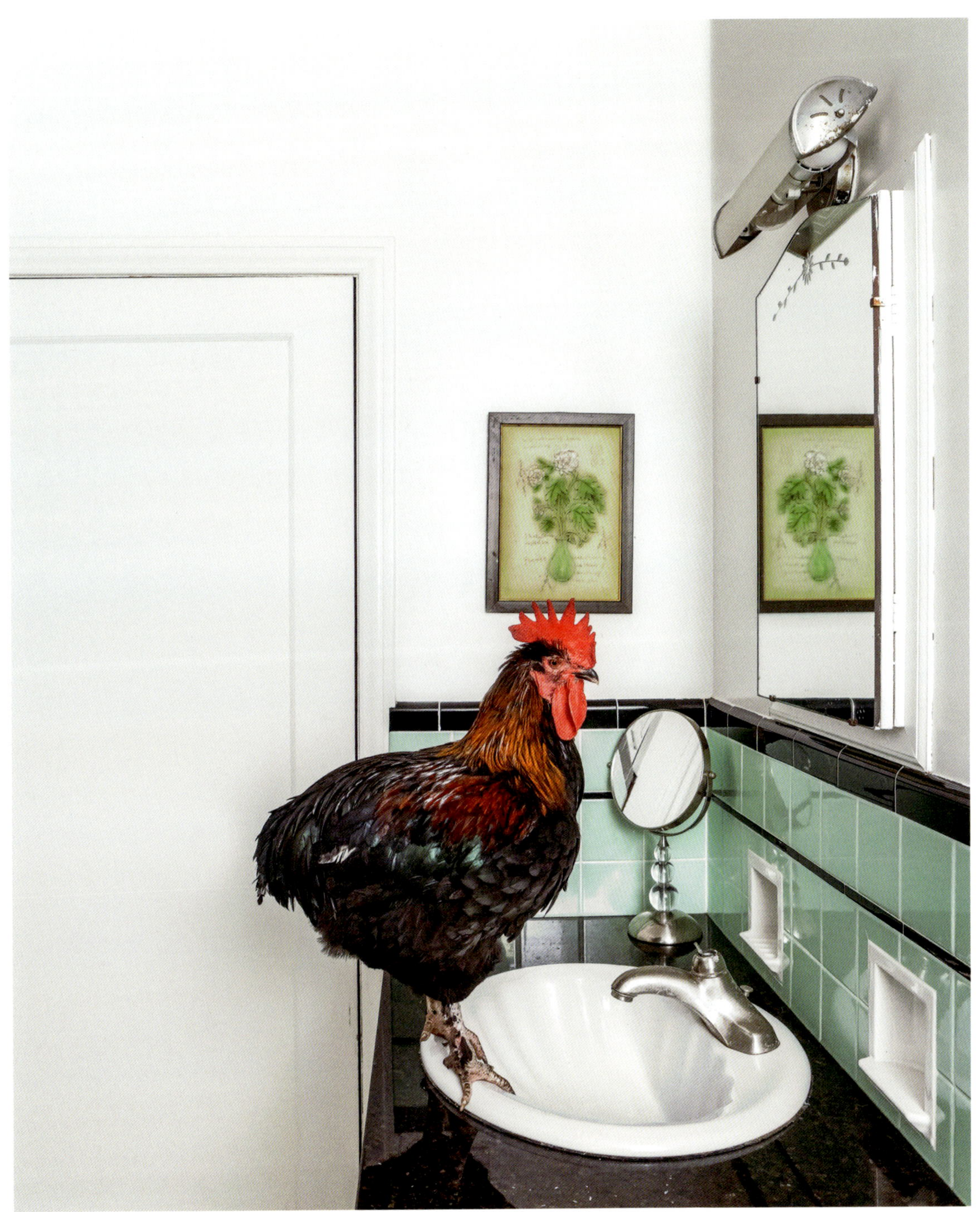

Roo June Brown

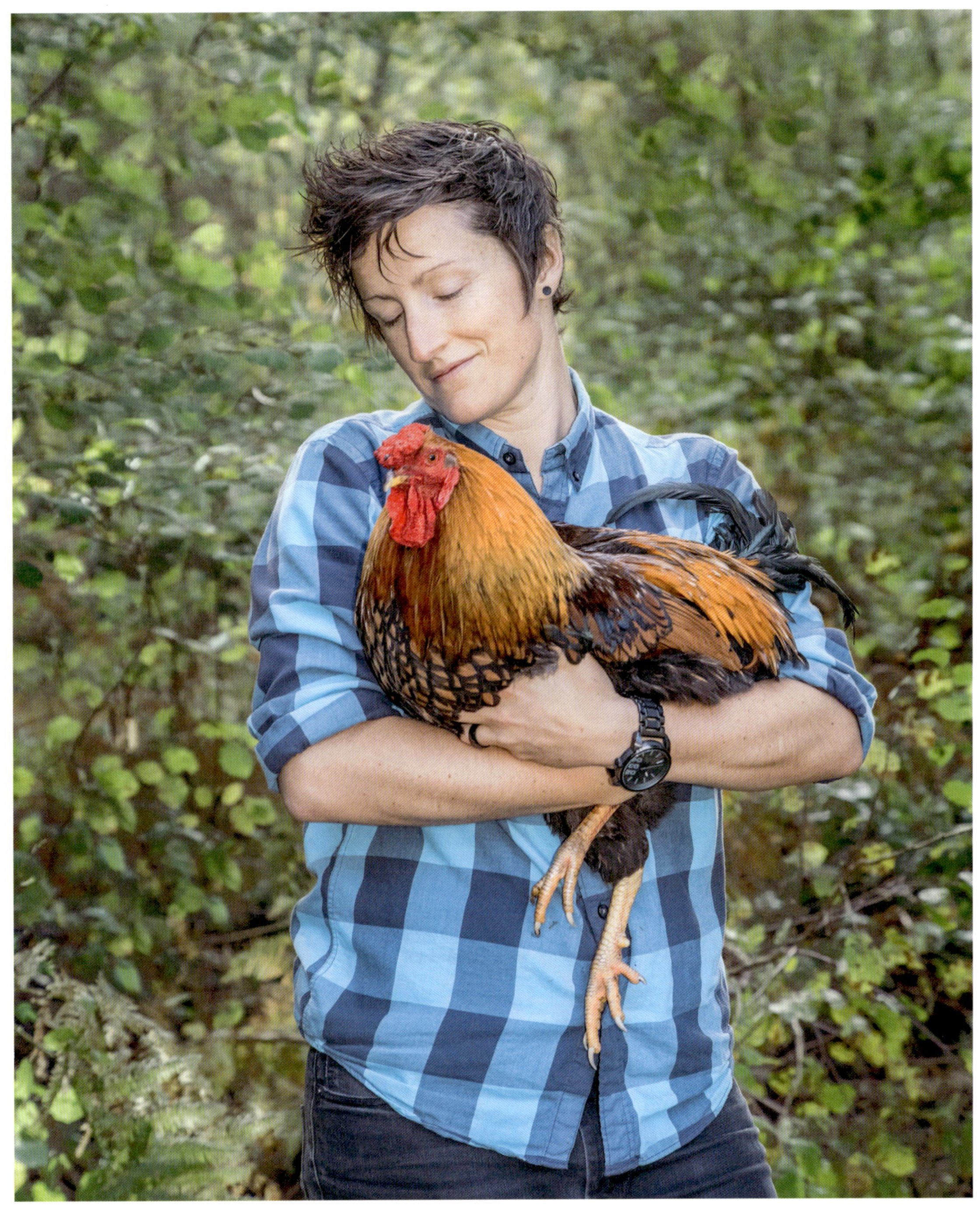

Monarch and Hope

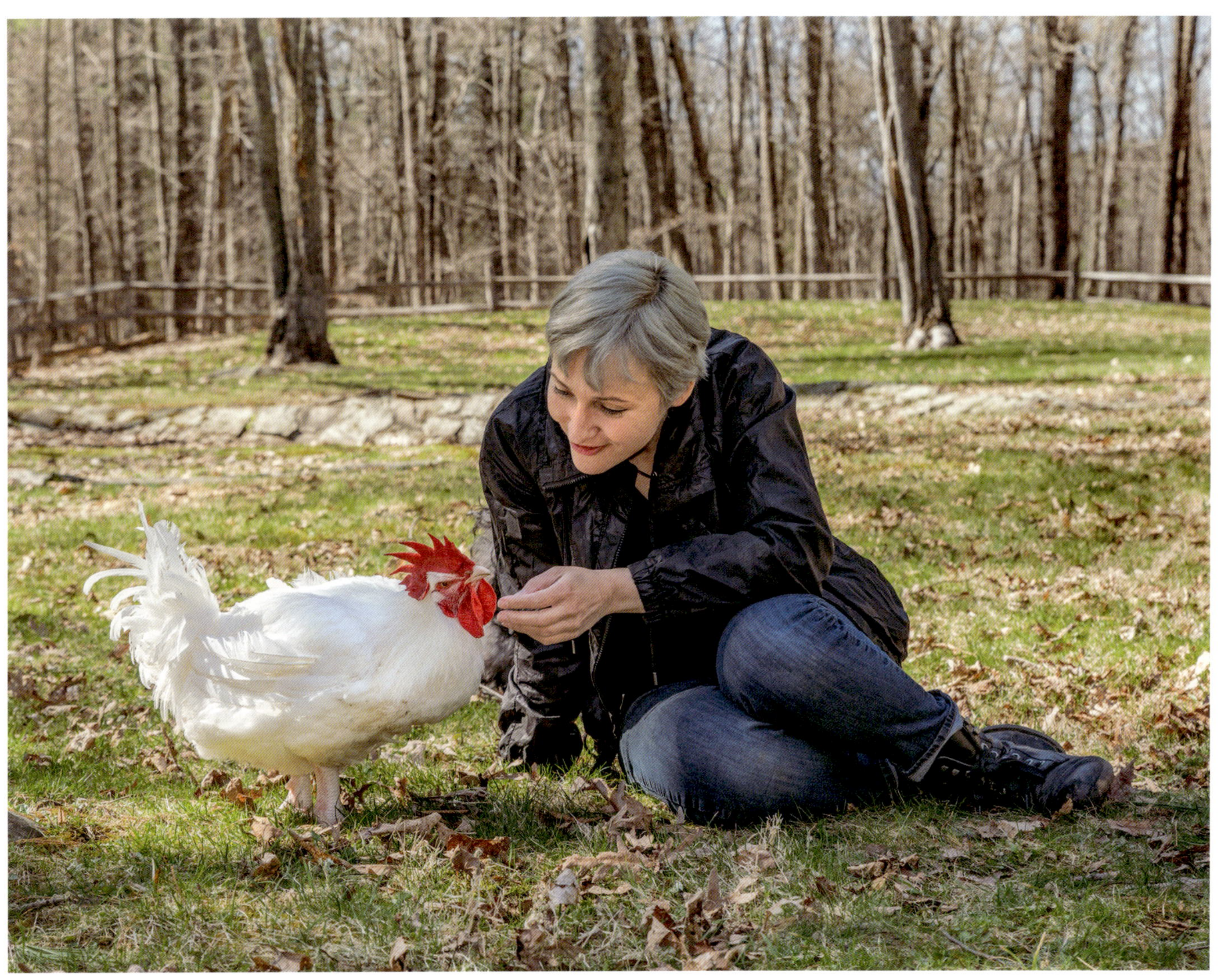

Buckles and Rebecca

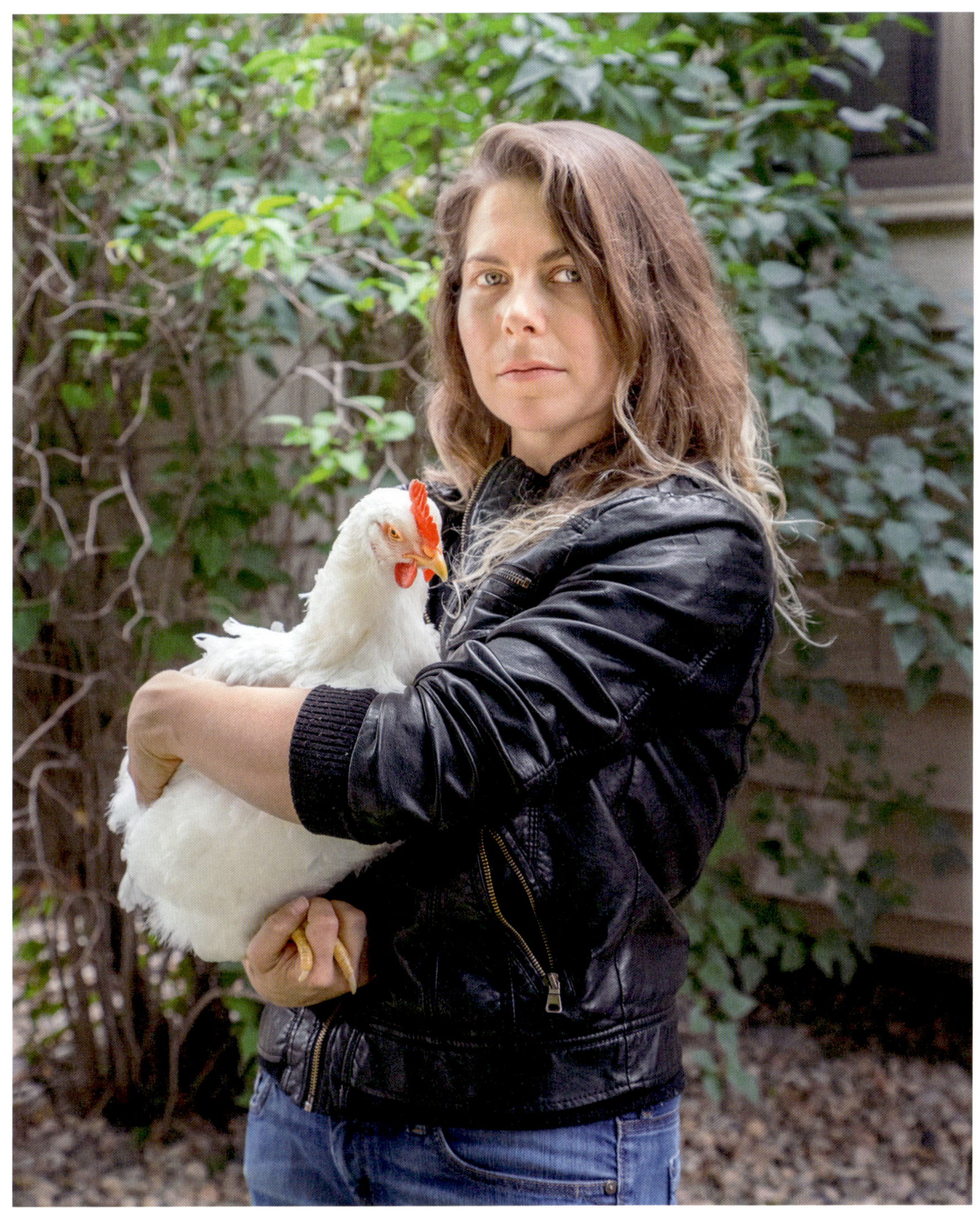

Alexa and Maddie

I was on a second date when I received an urgent phone call. A factory farm had gone bankrupt and tens of thousands of Cornish chicks were waiting for someone to come and either kill them or save them. A few hours later, a donor had paid for my plane ticket and several hours after that, I was on a plane with a suitcase full of medical supplies.

When I landed, I met up with two other rescuers. We drove to the nearest farm supply store and spent hundreds of dollars on tarps, carriers, duct tape, wood shavings for bedding, and other necessary supplies for rescue and transport.

We arrived at the farm in the afternoon. The farmer who met us was polite and trusting. It's scary for farmers to have activists on their property, but she was thankful we were there to save some of her animals. She said it was "better than the alternative."

The smell hit us before we entered the barn. Inside, there were tens of thousands of birds filling the entire space. It looked like every single undercover video I've ever seen. There was a chicken in front of me with a huge, bloody gash on their leg, struggling to walk. On my left, three small hens huddled together, weak and pale, next to the body of a friend who had already passed away. A few feet from them, several birds were hungrily tearing apart the dead body of another chick.

We started choosing the healthiest hens we could find, since they would have the best chance of surviving and being adopted. Roosters are harder to find homes for because some local governments don't allow roosters, and roosters sometimes fight if they are housed together without proper integration and supervision. I had to crouch down to look closely at their faces so that I could differentiate hens from roosters. At ground level, I saw birds with huge necrotic and bloody wounds, birds with horribly swollen faces and watery eyes, birds who were completely blind, and birds only a quarter the size of other birds their same age. They were dying all around us. The babies who were healthy enough to move formed massive cuddle puddles throughout the barn. Looking into the eyes of animals who needed help, knowing we had to leave thousands behind, was maddening and heartbreaking.

Farm workers walked past us to the back of the barn and began the killing. Meanwhile, we filled vehicles with hundreds of

individuals and drove to a nearby farm sanctuary, which was
providing emergency care. If we had it in us, we finally let ourselves cry in the vans. Getting emotional in front of the farm
workers was a danger to the rescue operation and not an option.

As sanctuary staff and local volunteers worked late into the
night taking care of the rescued individuals, three of us headed
to a nearby hotel to continue coordinating with other activists
across the country to secure more homes so that we could go
back and save more babies in the morning. We organized trans-
portation, foster families, fundraising, forever homes, and more
supplies. We finally went to bed around 2 or 3 a.m.

In the morning, we drank bad coffee, showered, and headed
back to the farm. Snow was falling outside, and inside the barn
felt freezing.

The killing crew had become too exhausted to finish breaking
necks the night before, so there were chickens left to save. I
picked up a tiny rooster who looked pale and sick and didn't
have the heart to put him back down. I picked up another chick
who was struggling to reach the frozen water lines. She's safe

now. I crouched down and looked over a group of huddled, cold little roosters. One turned and looked into my eyes. His face was horribly swollen and his eyes were cloudy, but he looked right at me. I left him behind.

We finally reached the number we had homes for, and then we overshot it, rescuing some we just couldn't bear to leave. I picked up a baby I had initially left behind, unsure if they were a rooster or a hen. I left behind a tiny one, head tucked into her back feathers, alone. I left behind another one who was snuggling between a bloody chicken who couldn't walk and a dead friend. We were standing in the middle of thousands of suffering animals, and it was impossible to save them all.

When I got to the car, I held that last baby I had liberated in my lap, and I wept.

————————————

Maddie Cartwright

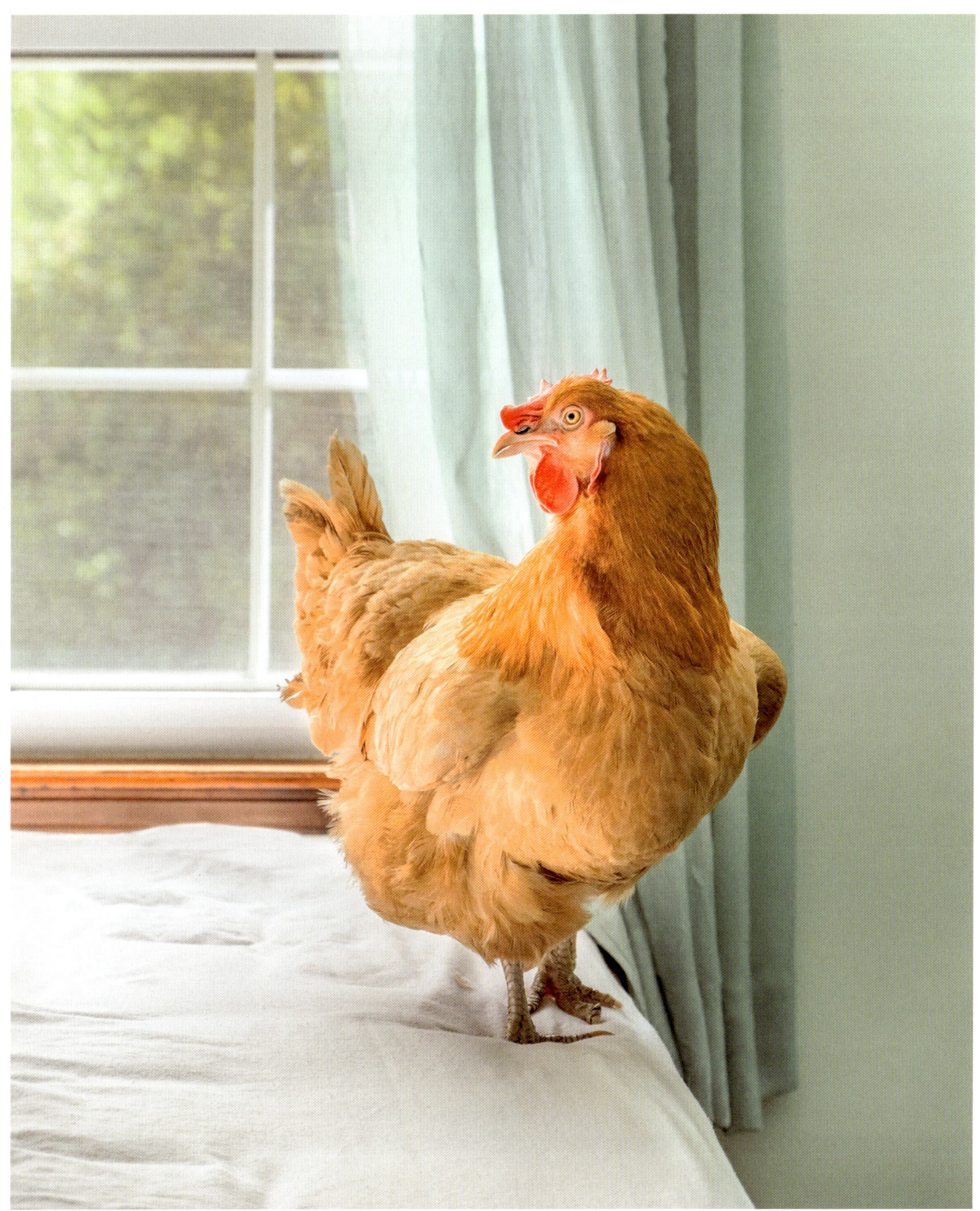

Valencia Jayne

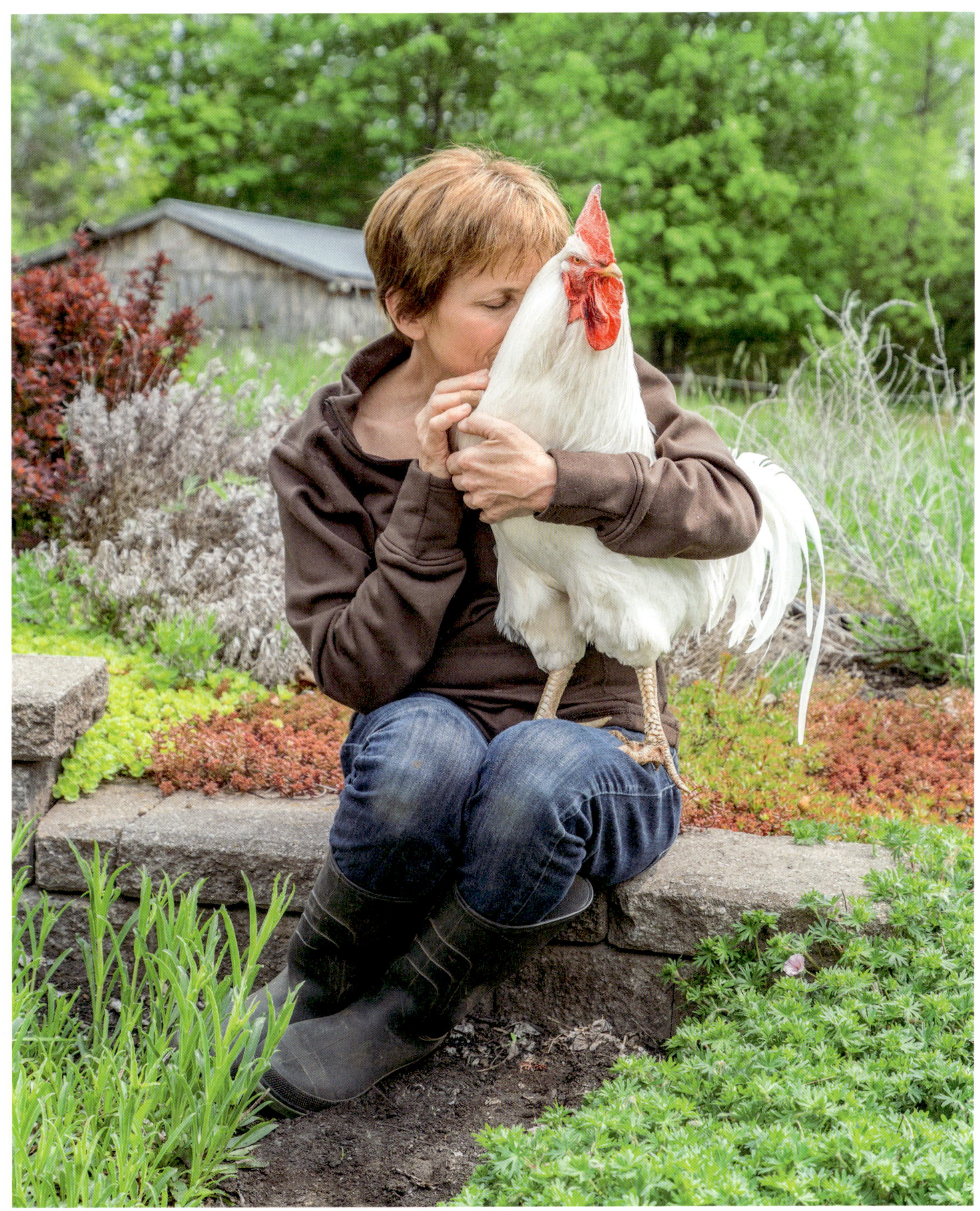

Lynn and Terror

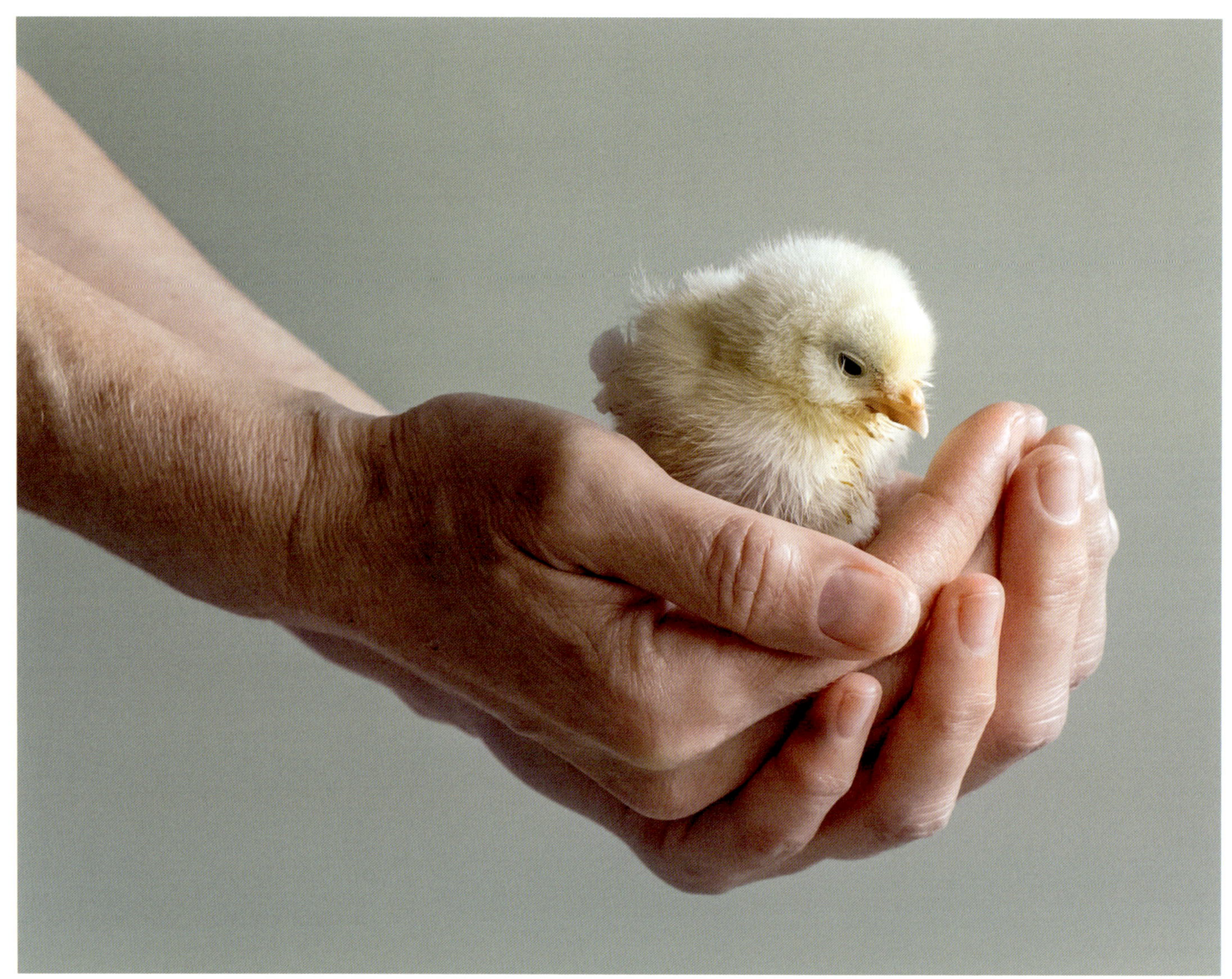

Sully

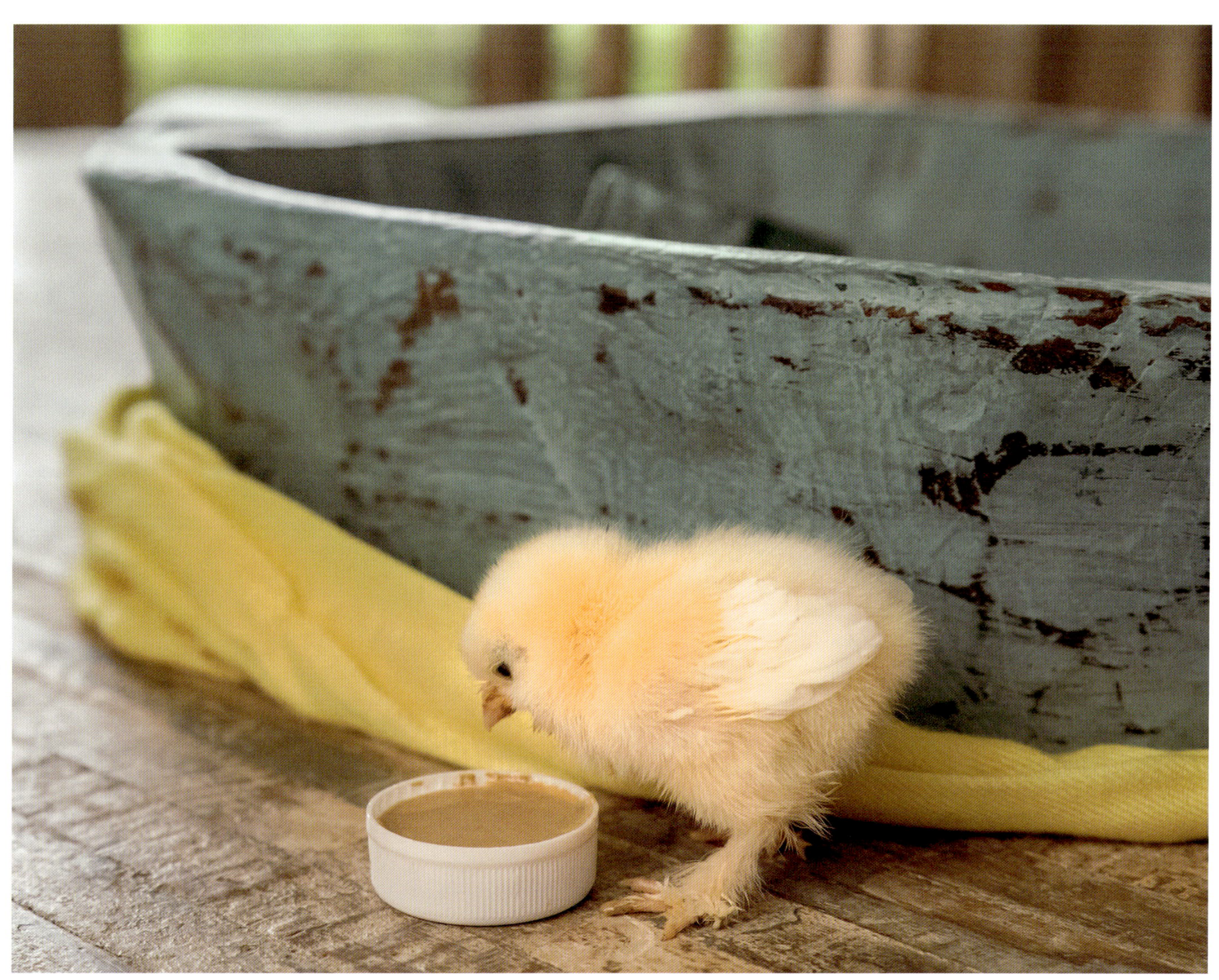

Sully

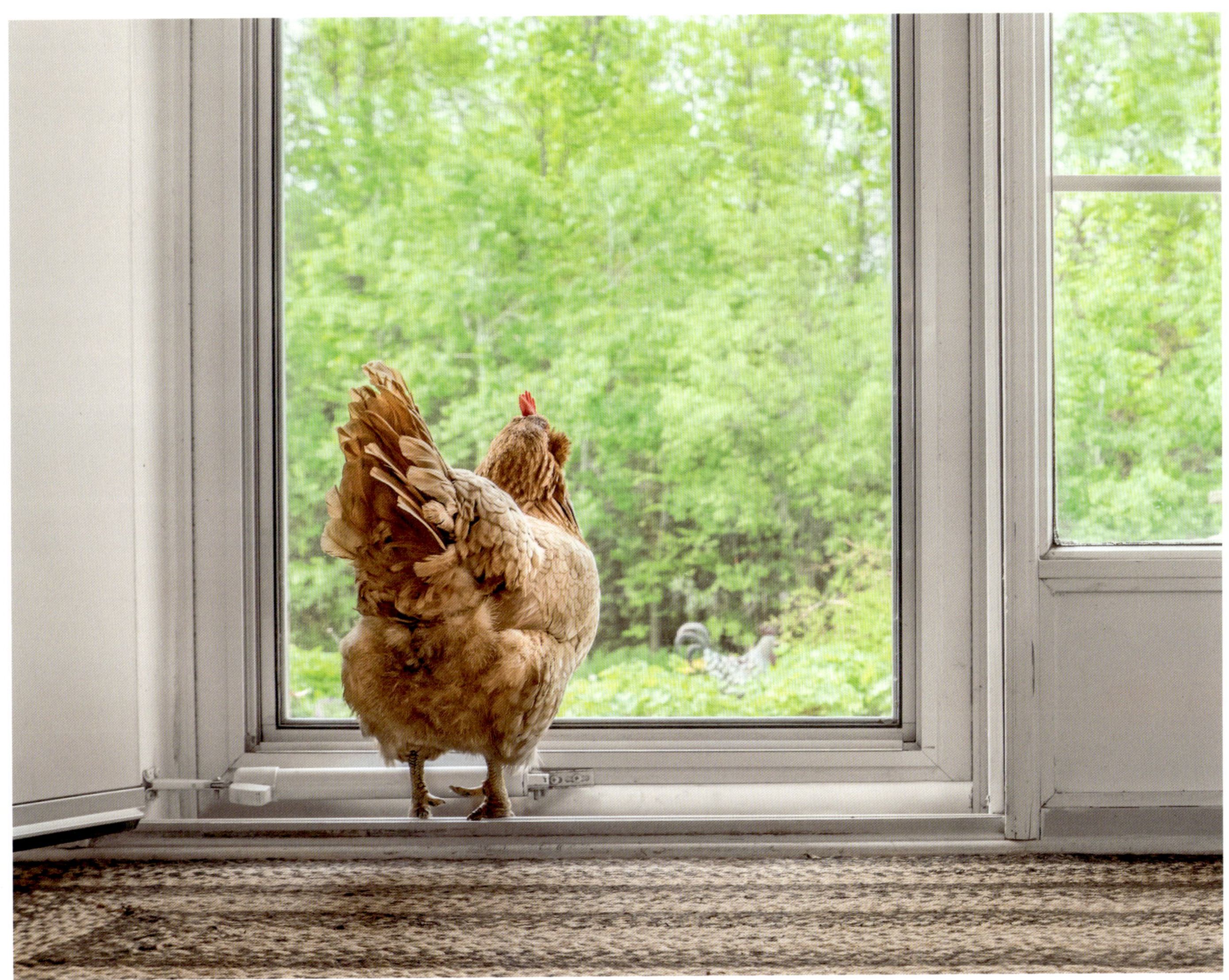

Colleen

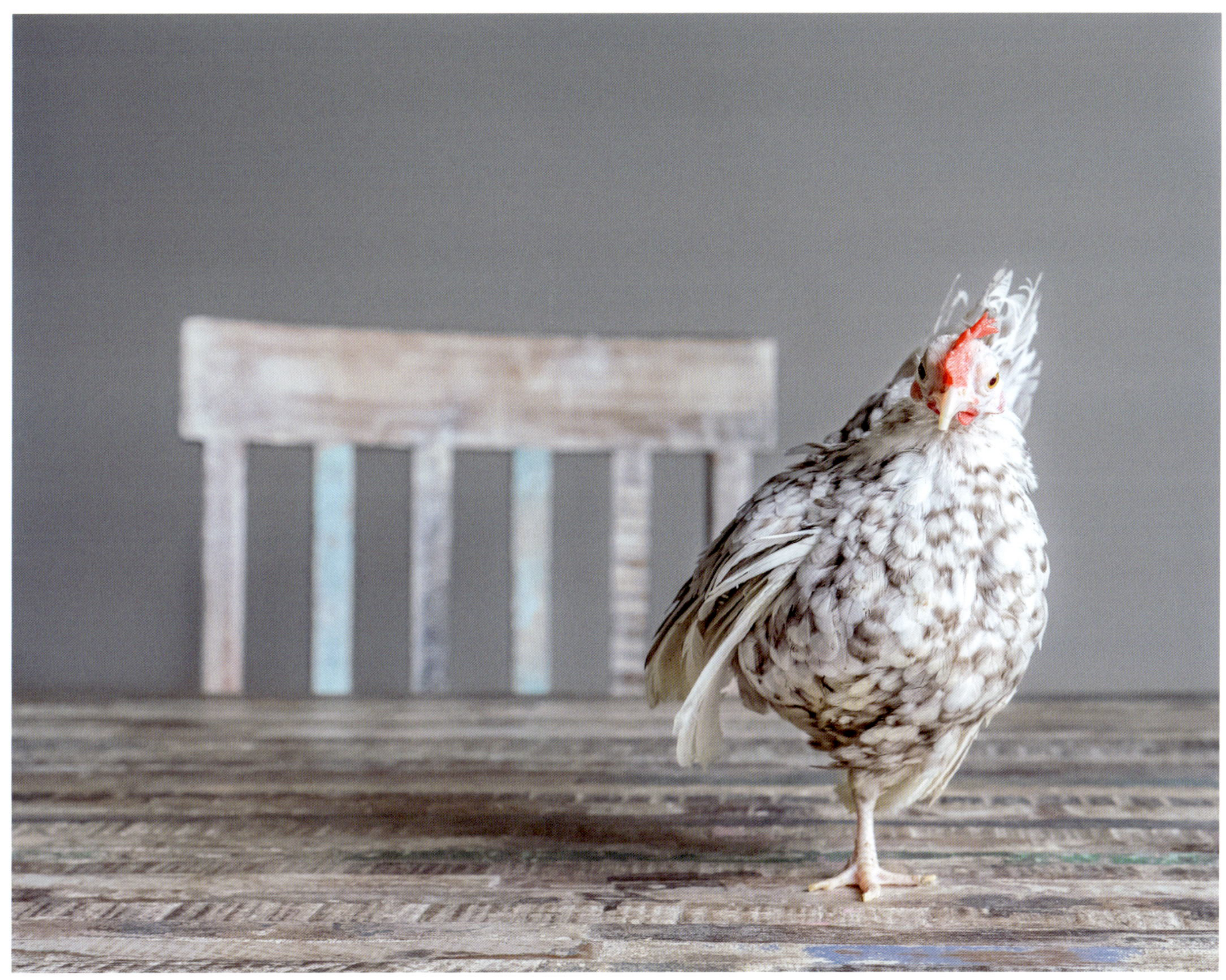

Flower

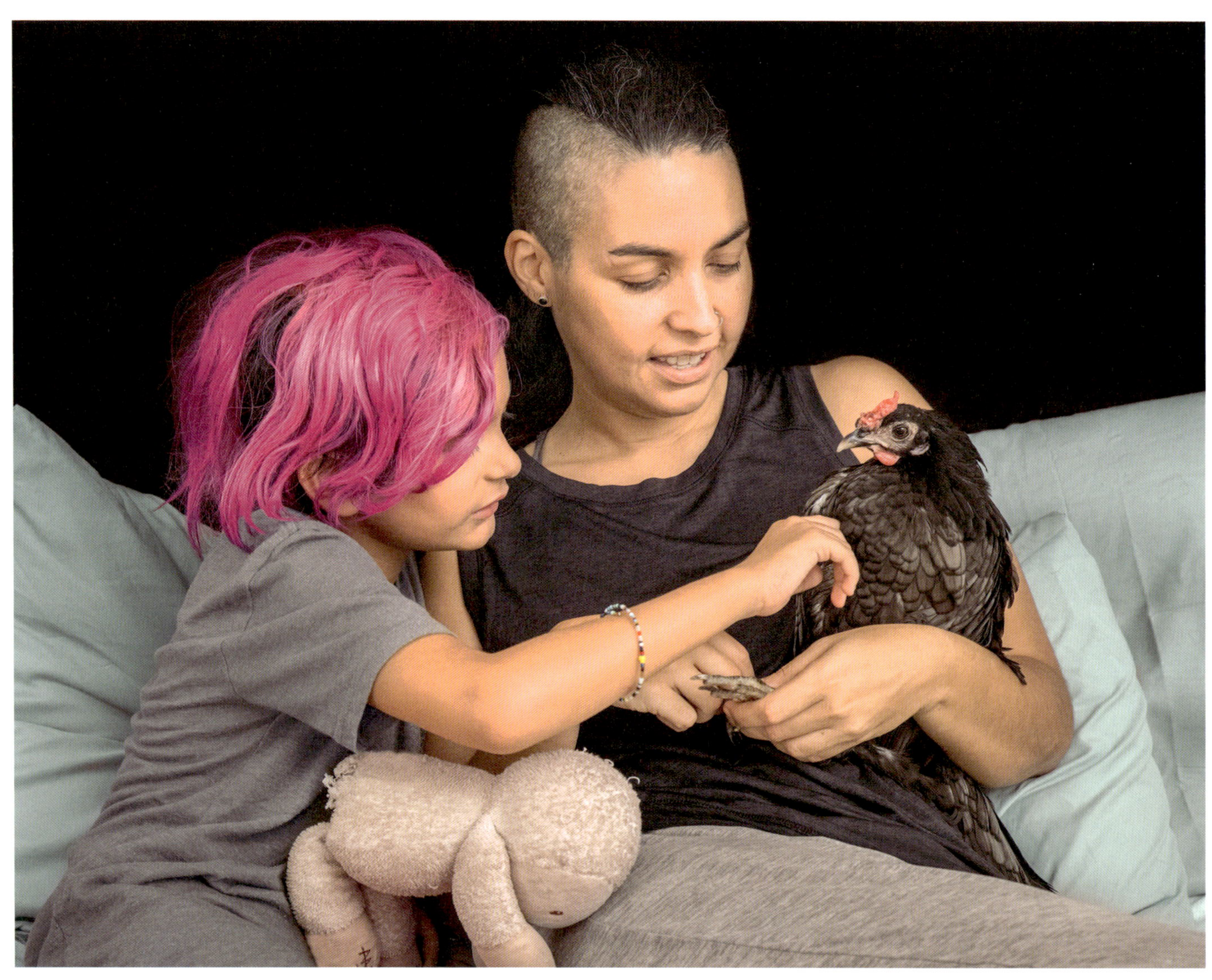

Ollie, Michelle, and Silencio

One hot day in Vega Baja, beside a drug den where we shared vegan food and drinks every Thursday, a guy showed up with a chick in his hand.

Miss, he was in a stray dog's mouth. I wrestled him out. What do I do now?

And that's how Silencio came into my life, and the lives of the hundreds of people who visit our Casa Vegana de la Comunidad in San Juan, Puerto Rico.

Silencio has grown up into a wonderful hen, who continues to amaze me in expressing who she is. She prefers tomatoes to spinach. She likes to have her fingers stroked, like she did when she was a baby and laid her hand in mine. She is happiest taking a dust bath where our house and the neighbor's wall meet. She loves to sit in visitors' laps, and yet she makes her boundaries clear and there are some days when she doesn't want cuddles.

I am a big believer in microsanctuaries for their ability to bring typically farmed animals into common humxn life. When people walk into our community house, the first people they meet are Silencio and Julia, our rescued rooster. They help bridge an emotional gap for folks used to seeing chickens in cages or as bodies to be consumed. It doesn't matter what brings a person into our center. They might come to explore the environmental, health, fitness, or ethical reasons for adopting a plant-based diet, but they leave having made a connection with a chicken. Silencio and Julia are our best spokespeople.

In a place like Puerto Rico, where I was born and raised, colonization is a lived experience. We have been colonized twice over, first by Spain, later by the United States. Chickens, too, have been colonized. They have been bred, held captive, objectified, depersonalized, commodified, and stripped of their nature.

Decolonizing ourselves starts with community. We find others who have been oppressed in similar ways, and then we come together to explore new ways of relating to each other and our world. Learning from one another, we create new visions of what can be.

For me, the process starts with decolonizing our diet. My indigenous ancestors lived mainly on a plant-based diet, supplemented with ocean people. Our first colonizers brought over chickens. Consuming their bodies and their eggs wasn't natural for my people. And yet now they are considered staples in our diet, at great cost to our health, the wellbeing of the non-humans themselves, and our connection to land and other species. Uniting humans to consider the myriad other ways that we and other animals have been colonized (economically, spiritually, sexually, culturally, and linguistically), while exploring how to return to our nature and liberate all beings from oppression, are the first steps in that process.

What does it mean for chickens then? The first step is to integrate them into our lives and connect with them in liberation. To be seen, to be acknowledged as a free person, is a powerful way to regain our own vision of our liberated selves.

And so we help humans see other species as free persons, while stopping ourselves from falling into saviorism. Just shifting from the view of animals as "things that we have to consume" to "things that we have to take care of" is another kind

of colonization, paternalistic and limited in scope and vision.
We must change the paradigm entirely. Chickens, and all other
species, are people with their own culture, and building a
community with them is the first step to free ourselves of the
oppression that has been handed down to us. We are not
people who need rescuing. We are people who deserve to be
free, to have sovereignty, to reconnect with who we are and
who we can be. We are figuring that out, in community, by
seeing each other, holding safe space to discover our free
selves, and practicing liberation together.

Michelle Carrera

Calendario de febrero
Lunes   Martes   Miercoles   Jueves   Viernes   Sabado   Domingo
1
2 Santurce Meal
3 Meal Prep Wkshp
4
5 Caguas Meal Share
6
7 Vega Baja Meal Share
8
9 Santurce Meal Share
10
11
12 Caguas Meal
13
14 Vega Baja meal Share
15
16 Santurce Meal Share
17 Niñxs Wkshp
18
21 Vega Baja meal Share
22
23 Santurce Meal
24 Vegan Fest
27
28 Vega Baja Meal Share
Caguas Meal Share
→ Traiga comida para el "Compra"
Chilis ON Wheels
Building community around free vegan food

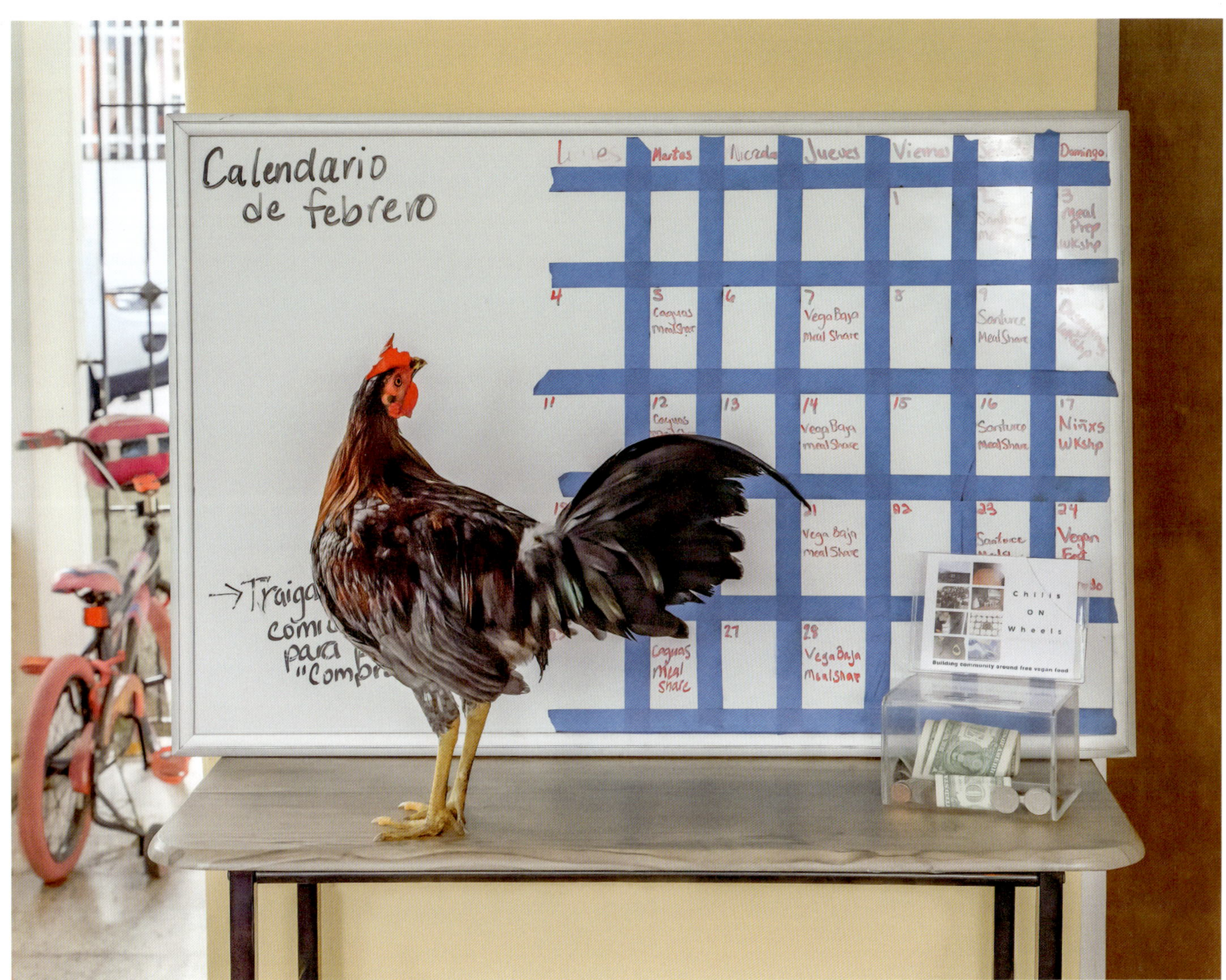

Julia

Kathy Stevens

Founder and

Executive Director,

Catskill Animal Sanctuary

Animals are part of my DNA. I was blessed to grow up on a thoroughbred breeding and training farm in Hanover County, Virginia, where my playmates, friends, and teachers were not only horses, but also a donkey named Linda, two precious goats, Babette the sheep, and too many dogs and cats to name here. Those early years allowed me to know for sure what became the foundational truth of Catskill Animal Sanctuary thirty years later: that in the ways that truly matter, we are all the same. In other words, the differences between human and non-animals say little about who we are as individuals and say nothing about how we should be treated. We all want our lives. Our basic needs are identical. We all have nuanced emotions that determine how we engage in the world. We are all remarkably individual: ten chickens are as different as ten children. And finally: pain, suffering, and terror feel no different to a chicken than they do to a child. Just because we live in a world that denies these obvious truths doesn't render them untrue.

Even with this understanding, I had much to learn when we opened Catskill Animal Sanctuary in 2001. Whether they came one by one or twenty at a time, when animals arrived generally they were *broken* — always physically, and often psychologically. Some were victims of profound neglect or outright cruelty. Others were lucky survivors of the meat and dairy industries who had never known a moment's kindness. At best, they were *extremely* wary of us. What a privilege it was to participate in the healing of wounded spirits — to watch as each one responded, at their own pace and on their own terms, to good food, soft words, the touch of kind hands.

Twenty years and 5,000 rescues later, I can say that except for life-altering experiences with Rambo the sheep, my greatest lessons have come from chickens. Dozens of larger-than-life personalities over the years have ensured that I appreciate the remarkable nature of the most abused animals on the planet. Paulie the former fighting rooster sprinted to us when we called his name, insisted on blueberries at lunch (and threw a tantrum if we humans didn't provide them), chased my car around the Sanctuary grounds demanding a ride in my lap, and gave the most wonderful hugs. Barbie the hen adored our sheep Rambo. Ignoring her flock of hens, she would awkwardly haul her big bird body on top of Rambo's back to nestle in for a nap. Sidra, an egg-industry survivor, is *obsessed* with laying her eggs in a bag of soft shavings stored in the barn kitchen. Her single-minded plotting to enter the kitchen even when we've blocked both the front and the back entrances and the cat door involves stealth, cunning, and dive-bombing unwitting volunteers as they open the door. Chickens, in other words, are most *definitely* "someones," and although science is finally documenting their astonishing intelligence, it's been obvious from the get-go to those of us lucky enough to work with them every day.

The power and promise of farm sanctuaries lie in our ability to help people see the "who-ness" of animals. When unsuspecting guests visit Catskill Animal Sanctuary, they are often met by disarmingly engaging animals: turkeys who want to climb in their laps or follow them around like a puppy would, cows who lick their faces over and over with their scratchy tongues, pigs who sprint to the fence when we call their names, and chickens who fall asleep in their arms. Sanctuaries know the impact of these moments. We witness the tears that often accompany them or hear words like the ones from a recent visitor, who, overcome, took my forearms in his hands and with tears streaming down his face said simply, "I get it now. Please tell me what to do." We humans may offer a *damned* good tour, but the animals are our most impactful activists.

And yet one needn't "go big" to be an advocate for animals. While some people run sanctuaries, organize street protests, or document unspeakable cruelty at farms and slaughterhouses, others engage in a deceptively powerful form of activism by living with chickens, ducks, or turkeys. Camille Licate not only loves her rooster Bree every bit as much as I love my dogs Chumbley and Scout; Bree opens the heart and mind of everyone who encounters him. When he runs affectionately to Camille, responds to his name, communicates what he wants with a vast array of sounds, nestles into someone's lap, or trots down the stairs of the house as deftly as an athletic child, we're forced not only to confront the terrible inaccuracy of our perceptions, but also the harm we inflict when we relegate all members of his species to "food." In these moments, both precious and uncomfortable, Bree and others like him become game-changing ambassadors for their species. So for the people featured in this book and others around the world who share their homes with "food animals," care in and of itself is a powerful form of activism.

So, too, is the photography of Janet Holmes. When she visits Catskill Animal Sanctuary to photograph our residents, she knows exactly how to be with them. She sits among the horses and cows, the chickens and sheep, the turkeys and pigs and goats in our barns, our lanes, our pastures. She waits for them to come to her, inviting them to smell, touch, nibble, and experience her. The animals trust her quiet energy; they hide nothing from her. The results speak for themselves in breathtaking portraits of our beloved friends. And although I haven't had the privilege of seeing Janet photograph the families featured in this book, the photos themselves tell me all I need to know. The chickens trusted Janet, and that trust allowed her to make these exquisite images that invite us to understand rare and powerful truths about a misunderstood, underappreciated species, and about the universal capacity for love.

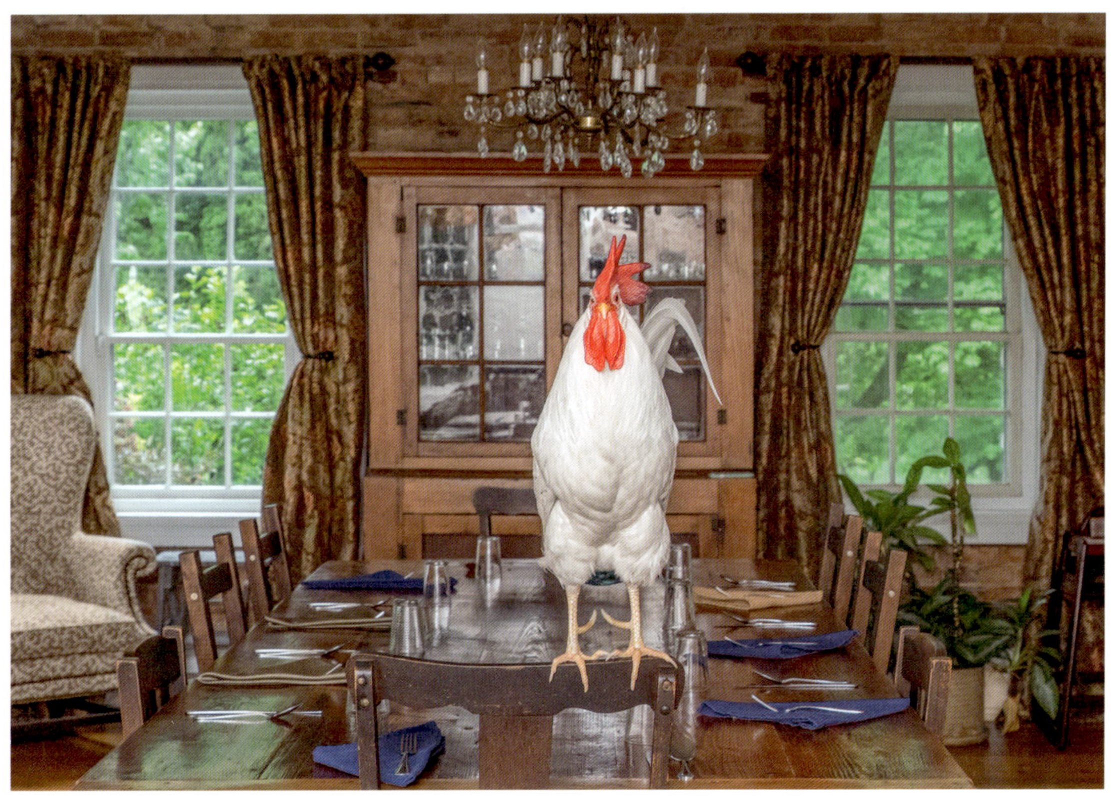

Bree on a visit to Catskill Animal Sanctuary

Janelle Lynch

Faculty, International Center

of Photography

Nadine and Shelley are out for a stroll along a path of fragrant flora. Winnie is just back from her own outing. Valencia Jayne, afoot on fresh linens, is flanked by green curtains that complement her red wattle. Where else should such a radiant creature rest?

The invitation to consider animals as sentient beings has been offered many times before. In my personal library alone there are *The Truro Bear and Other Adventures*, Mary Oliver's poems and essays about the beasts she revered; Colleen Plumb's *Animals Are Outside Today*, fine art photographs that contemplate humans' impact on other living beings; and John Berger's *Why Look at Animals*, an examination of "the evolution of our relationship with animals and how they went from muses… to spiritual deities to captive entertainment."[1] Janet Holmes' *Nest: Rescued Chickens at Home*, a book of portraits of chickens and chickens with their caregivers is an inspiring addition.

"Penelope, Vanessa, Alicia, and Jenny" is an environmental portrait of a woman and three chickens in a parquet-floored living room. Adorned with a rocking chair, soft natural light, Buddha statues, and Tibetan singing bowls, the space suggests a sanctuary for all. "Josie and Rachel" depicts a woman reclining on a white sofa, draped by a big black and white bird and an orange throw. The woman is at rest, eyes closed, while the chicken nestles alertly in her arm. The caretaking is reciprocal. That the titles of the pictures give no indication of who the guardian is suggests Holmes' conception about the animals in relation to their human counterparts, and underscores her intention to ask us, the viewer, to consider our similarities to chickens, despite the obvious differences. Knowing Holmes as a devoted activist, I am confident that her request applies to all animals — goats, geese, horses, hogs. And beyond.

Those were, in fact, the subject of Holmes' images when I met her in the spring of 2015 at the International Center of Photography where, following a growing interest in the medium, she had been studying since 2014. By then she had already acquired the strong technical foundation and understanding of photography's visual language that would form the basis of her work as an award-winning animal activist photographer. A Canadian-born securities lawyer, Holmes was, by day, working for a multinational company headquartered in New York City. Following a lifelong appreciation of animals, it was natural, if not inevitable, for her to focus on animals in her photography coursework. "I've always loved them," she told me recently. "I was that kid who wrecked her dress crawling under a pickup truck to say hello to a garter snake."

Devoted equally to the craft as she was to the animals, Holmes continued honing her skills, taking master classes in printing and portraiture until 2017.

Concurrent with her studies at ICP, Holmes began volunteering for rescue groups, including the Wild Bird Fund and Mighty Mutts in New York City, and Catskill Animal Sanctuary in Saugerties, New York. "As I spent more time experiencing animals as a caregiver and photographer, I began to question how I could profess to love them yet continue to exploit them for food and clothing." She committed to veganism and to using photography to advocate for animal liberation.

Since 2015, when she self-published her first book, *Love and Healing at Catskill Animal Sanctuary*, she has been exhibiting her images throughout the country. Now based in Toronto, she continues both practices — lawyering and photographing — the latter of which is conducted primarily on a non-profit basis. Holmes donates her services and at least half of her profits from print sales to support animal rescue.

The images Holmes was making at Catskill Animal Sanctuary when we met in 2015 were so powerful in their ability to convey animals as sentient creatures, with personalities and intelligence, that I was compelled to return to vegetarianism. She, like Plumb, whose aforementioned book includes the image "Chickens in Crab Traps", often photographs at her subject's eye level. For both photographers, this approach comes from a place of empathy and is used as a means to evoke empathy in the viewer.

Three years later, in 2018, due to the indelible resonance of Holmes' work, I visited the Sanctuary. There I met several of the animals — Callie, Bea, and Omar, among others — whom Holmes had skillfully and compassionately photographed while studying at ICP. It was after that experience that I, too, committed to veganism. I am thankful to Holmes for the introduction to it all — the beautiful animals, the extraordinary place, founded by Kathy Stevens, and the lifestyle that is aligned with my values.

Until the 1800s, anthropomorphism was "integral to the relation between man and animal," Berger notes in *Why Look at Animals*. He quotes Aristotle's *History of Animals* to show how far we as a culture have moved away from such an appreciation of their complex nature, "for just as we pointed out resemblances in the physical organs, so in a number of animals we observe gentleness and fierceness, mildness or cross-temper, courage or timidity, fear or confidence, high spirits or low cunning, and, with regard to intelligence, something akin to sagacity."

I recall conversations at ICP with Holmes about anthropomorphism. Only now in retrospect do I realize that the photographer wasn't then attributing humanlike characteristics to the non-human animals in her images; she was acknowledging that what we often call "human" traits are qualities that exist across species. And she was doing so then, as she does in *Nest: Rescued Chickens at Home*, with reverence and a hint of humor. For example, in "Cluckey," the bird is shown standing in front of an open refrigerator, likely — following my own personal experience doing the same — not even hungry.

Similar to those of her animal activist peers — photographers including Jo-Anne McArthur, Mary Shannon Johnstone, and Martin Usborne — Holmes' images are imbued with appreciation and the belief that animals are here with us, not for us. Her perspective is informed by a devotion to basic rights — the sensibility that led her first to the field of law. Before she begins photographing, she invites the animals to be with her on their own terms. She acknowledges that an animal cannot consent to be photographed, so she attunes herself to their behavior. If an animal indicates discomfort, Holmes won't photograph them. While some animal photography actually contributes to animal exploitation — on game farms, for example — and some reinforces the social norms that value animals for how they please humans by showcasing those bred for beauty, Holmes honors the creature foremost. There is no objectification here.

Thus, in this book, we meet a variety of birds — speckled ones, balding ones, even a chick — and on two occasions, their canine companions, which brings me back to Mary Oliver, who wrote plenty about her own dogs, though never about a chicken. If she did, the poem would have been invested with the same respect and celebratory spirit that Holmes conveys in her photographs.

Artful, amusing, and tender, Holmes' portraits are a tribute to the caregivers and birds, as well as to those who met other, much less fortunate fates. In *Nest: Rescued Chickens at Home*, she, like the other authors whose books stand in my library, extends an invitation to viewers to reconsider their perception of and relation to animals — one that I gratefully accept.

1   Maria Popova, "Why Look at Animals: John Berger on What Our Relationship with Our Fellow Beings Reveals About Us," *Brainpickings*, accessed March 3, 2020, https://www.brainpickings.org/2014/04/01/why-look-at-animals-john-berger-about-looking.

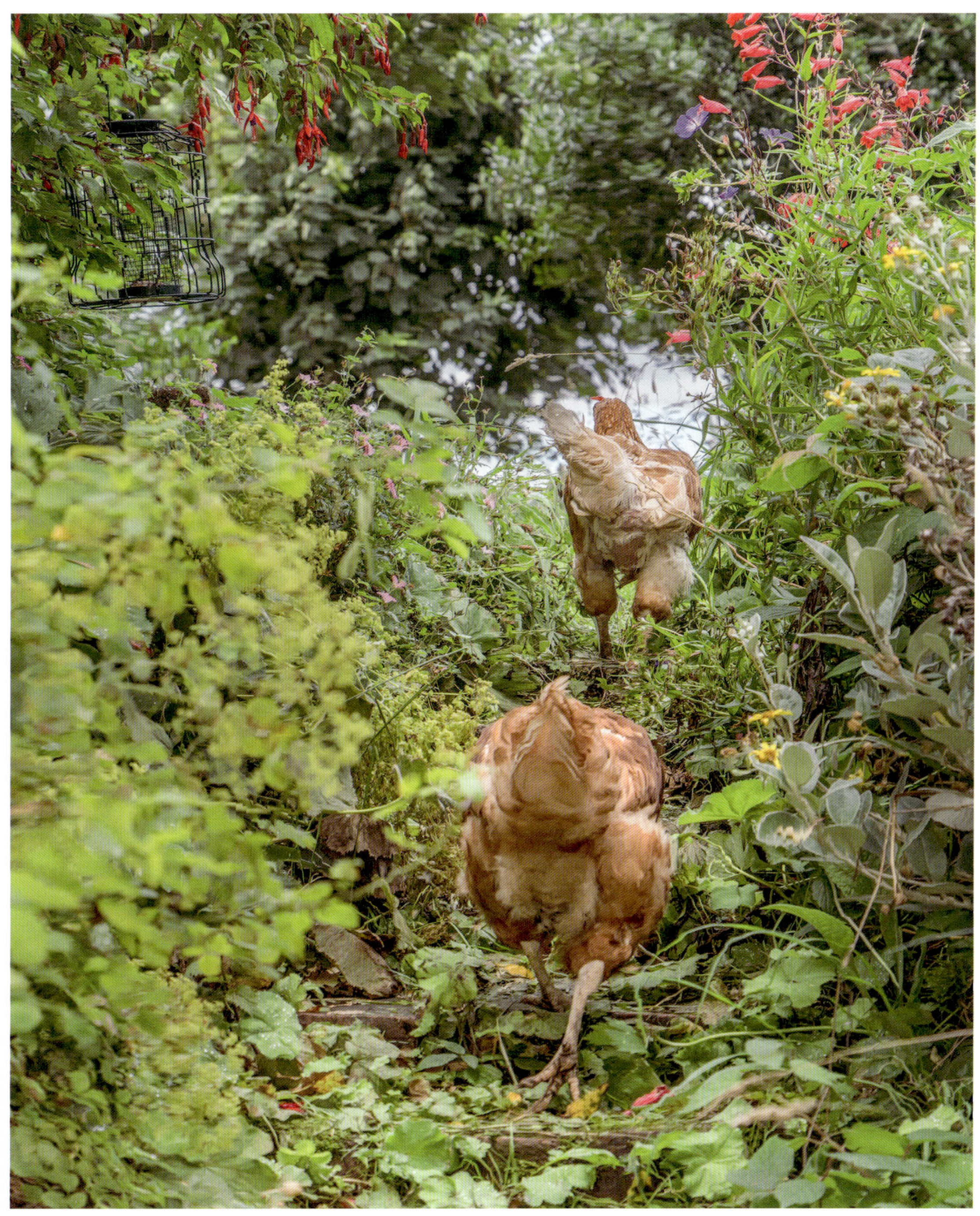

Nadine and Shelley

Acknowledgments

To the chickens and humans I have photographed, thank you for welcoming me into your homes, for showing me how wonderful chickens are, and for allowing me to experience some of the love, redemption, laughter, and grief that is part of caring for neglected, abused, and abandoned hens and roosters.

I am grateful to the following humans for permitting me to include portraits of them and / or their beloved companions in this book: Rachel Arima (Hens of the Hills); Kelsey Atkinson; Jennifer Bafile; Jessica Barhitte; Rachel Bee (Daisy View Microsanctuary); Temara Brown (The Browns' Microsanctuary); Michelle and Ollie Carrera (Casa Vegana de la Comunidad); Maddie Cartwright; Chicago Chicken Rescue; Mel Conway-Lusted (New Hope Farm Sanctuary); Vanessa Dawson (Penelope's Place: The Sanctuary); Mahika Gupta; Hope Hilman and Katya Tsyrklevich (Heartwood Haven Vegan Animal Sanctuary); Rachel Hipp (Sanctuary Moon: Home for Animals); Lynn Kennedy (Contented Clucks Farm Sanctuary); Kelly Landreth; Camille Licate; Julia Magnus and Cosmos Ray Boekell (Chicago Roo Crew); Elaine Maltezos (Bergen Chicken Sanctuary); Quincy Markowitz (Farm Bird Sanctuary); Rehana Mohammed-Smith (Georgia's Place Bird Sanctuary); Rebecca Moore (Institute for Animal Happiness); April Noga; Jade Norby (Xanadu All-Beings Sanctuary); Katrina Perkowsa (Kasia's Ark Bird Rescue); Jenny Rae (Rooster Haus Rescue); Nikki Rae; Rocky Schwartz; Ashley Snyder; Gabrielle Williams-Soeldner; and Kelly Witwicki.

To the community of vegans who provide sanctuary, and / or advice to others providing sanctuary, to chickens, thank you for sharing your knowledge with caregivers and me, for supporting each other emotionally and financially, and for inspiring people to provide safe, nurturing homes for birds in need. I'm especially grateful to the Microsanctuary Resource Center (microsanctuaryresourcecenter.org), which publishes care guides for different species, moderates online discussion groups for caregivers, and provides grants to caregivers including a fund to help people pay for contraceptive and other reproductive health care services for chickens.

I am also very grateful to Michelle Carrera, Maddie Cartwright, Julia Magnus, Rocky Schwartz, and Ashley Snyder for their lyrical memoirs and to Kathy Stevens and Janelle Lynch for the wonderful essays that they have contributed to this book. Thank you as well to my team at Kehrer Verlag, including Alexa Becker, Julia Frohnhoff, Tom Grace, Patrick Horn, Loreen Lampe, and of course, Klaus Kehrer, for believing in this book and helping me bring my vision to fruition.

And finally, I want to thank my family (especially my husband Miles O'Reilly, sister Cathy, father Bill Holmes, and mother-in-law Joan O'Reilly) who have listened patiently to me as I talked endlessly about chickens and chicken portraits, driven me to photo sessions, provided feedback on images and texts, and supplied coffee, financial support, and encouragement whenever I needed it.

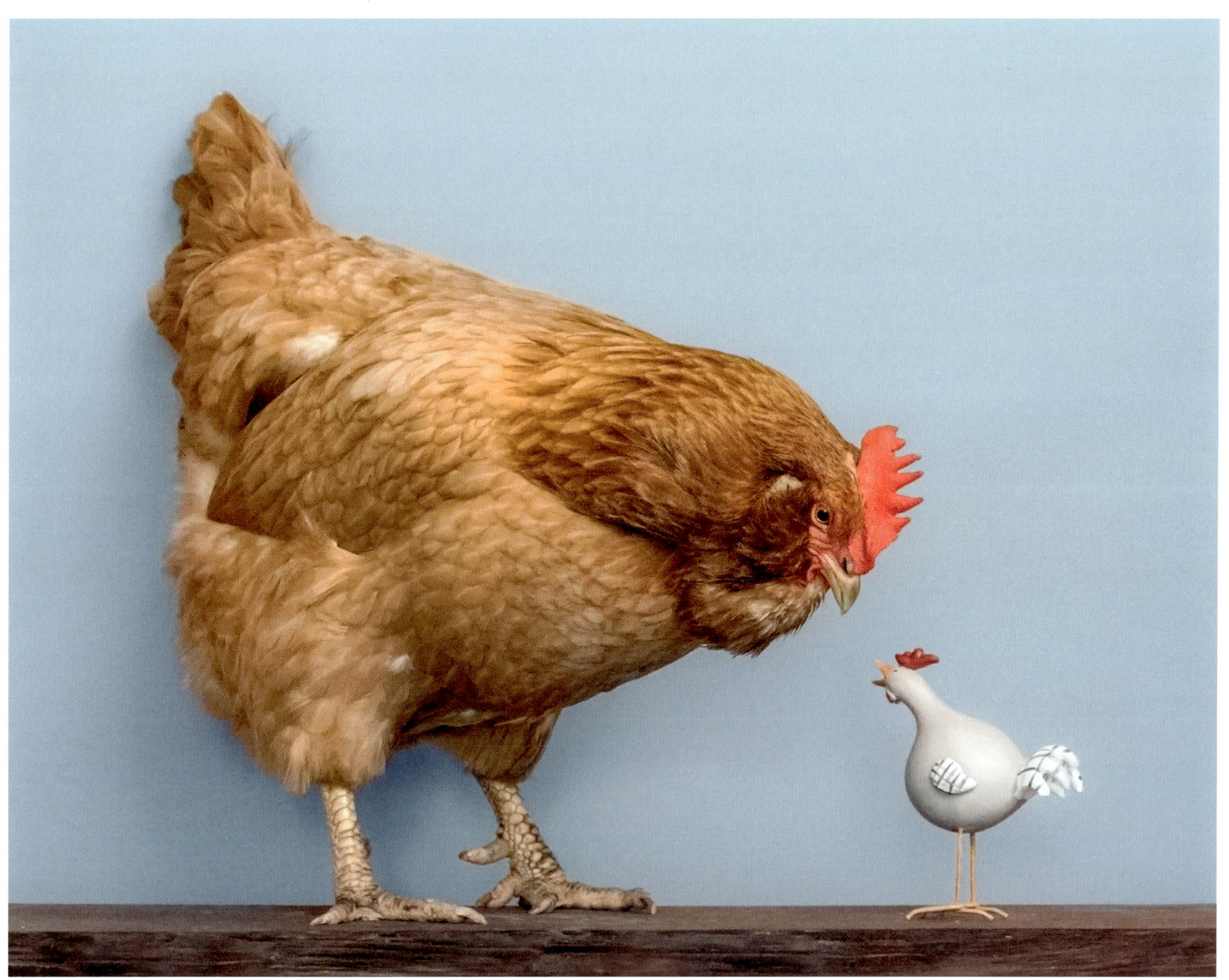

Colleen and Friend

PHOTOGRAPHS AND INTRODUCTION
Janet Holmes

ESSAYS
Janelle Lynch, Kathy Stevens

MEMOIRS
Michelle Carrera, Maddie Cartwright,
Julia Magnus, Rocky Schwartz, Ashley Snyder

PROJECT MANAGEMENT
Kehrer Verlag (Julia Frohnhoff)

COPY EDITING
Tom Grace

DESIGN
Kehrer Design (Loreen Lampe)

IMAGE PROCESSING
Kehrer Design (Patrick Horn)

PRODUCTION MANAGEMENT
Kehrer Design (Tom Streicher)

BIBLIOGRAPHIC INFORMATION
published by the Deutsche Nationalbibliothek:
The Deutsche Nationalbibliothek lists this publication in
the Deutsche Nationalbibliografie; detailed bibliographic
data is available on the Internet at http://dnb.dnb.de.

Printed and bound in Germany
ISBN 978-3-86828-987-9

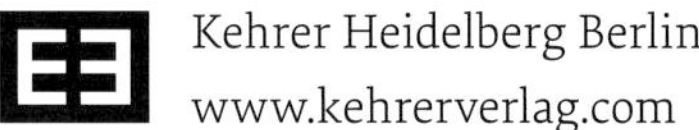
Kehrer Heidelberg Berlin
www.kehrerverlag.com